Canine Cuisine

Visit our How To website at www.howto.co.uk

At **www.howto.co.uk** you can engage in conversation with our authors – all of whom have 'been there and done that' in their specialist fields. You can get access to special offers and additional content but most importantly you will be able to engage with, and become a part of, a wide and growing community of people just like yourself.

At **www.howto.co.uk** you'll be able to talk and share tips with people who have similar interests and are facing similar challenges in their lives. People who, just like you, have the desire to change their lives for the better – be it through moving to a new country, starting a new business, growing their own vegetables, or writing a novel.

At **www.howto.co.uk** you'll find the support and encouragement you need to help make your aspirations a reality.

You can go direct to www.canine-cuisine.co.uk which is part of the main How To site.

How To Books strives to present authentic, inspiring, practical information in their books. Now, when you buy a title from **How To Books,** you get even more than just words on a page.

Canine Cuisine

Elaine Everest

howtobooks

Published by How To Books Ltd,
Spring Hill House, Spring Hill Road,
Begbroke, Oxford OX5 1RX
Tel: (01865) 375794. Fax: (01865) 379162
info@howtobooks.co.uk
www.howtobooks.co.uk

How To Books greatly reduce the carbon footprint of their books by sourcing their typesetting and printing in the UK.

First edition 2010

British Library Cataloguing in Publication Data
A catalogue record for this book is available from the British Library

ISBN: 978-1-84528-408-4

Cartoons © Colin Shelbourn, www.shelbourn.com
Produced for How To Books by Deer Park Productions, Tavistock
Typeset by PDQ Typesetting Ltd, Newcastle-under-Lyme
Printed and bound by Bell & Bain Ltd, Glasgow

NOTE: The material contained in this book is set out in good faith for general guidance and no liability can be accepted for loss or expense incurred as a result of relying in particular circumstances on statements made in the book. The laws and regulations are complex and liable to change, and readers should check the current position with the relevant authorities before making personal arrangements.

Contents

v

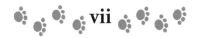

Acknowledgements

Simple, I thought, as I opened the first page on my computer and headed it 'Canine Cuisine'. Writing about feeding a dog and listing recipes would be a doddle. I have dogs and I cook so what could be simpler? It was then that I realised how complex the world of dog food has become. By advising dog owners to make their own, would I be jumped on one dark night and harassed by large corporations who make a fortune from selling brightly coloured dog food? Would the 'feed raw food' campaigners beat me to death with a leg of lamb? As I researched the subject and spoke to dog owners I began to realise that there is a place for all food providers and we, as owners, must make up our own minds when it comes to feeding our beloved pets.

Thank you to all the dog owners from The Write Place who have given me feedback on the dietary likes and dislikes of their four-legged charges.

I would like to dedicate this book to my husband Michael who on more than one occasion arrived home and announced, 'That smells good, what's for dinner?' only to find I'd been testing a recipe on our dogs. They had best steak and he visited the chip shop!

Finally, my faithful Old English Sheepdogs Peggy, Nelson, Buster, Squidgy and Molly who were my official food tasters, and not forgetting our much missed Gracie and William waiting at The Rainbow Bridge.

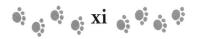

xi

Why Cook for Our Dogs?

There has been much discussion in recent years as to the suitability of some mass-produced dog food. In the same way that we consider what we put onto our own dinner plates, we should be wondering what exactly our dogs are eating when we open sacks of brightly coloured animal feed or pick up a can opener to feed Fido an unknown meat covered in jelly.

The cost of dog food is astronomical and as we all have to watch the pennies when we shop it is easy to fall into the trap of purchasing cheaper pet food. This can be a false economy as cheap is not usually good and we need to feed more or our dogs become thin. The ingredients may not be the best available and our dogs will not thrive. A sick dog will mean more trips to the vet, and we all know that there is no such thing as a poor vet!

By cooking your dog's food from scratch you are in control of what goes in and what comes out. I'm appalled by some dog food which boasts that there's less appearing out the dog's rear end and that their food also controls the odour when a dog defecates. It's not natural!

For those of us who already cook rather than relying on convenience foods for our families, we know that not only are we healthier but our weekly shopping bills are lower. So why not try the same when feeding your dog? It may take a little planning but sitting down once a week and writing a menu will not take long. Food can be made in bulk and frozen. Doggy biscuits and treats can also be made in batches and stored in airtight containers.

Weights and Measures

I've tried to make each recipe as easy to follow as possible. We should all be enjoying our dog's company, not sweating over a hot stove. Not all of us own large amounts of cooking equipment so I've kept to the basics. Most recipes include measurements in mugs – we all have a coffee mug in our cupboard so it is an easy measuring implement. Take hold of a large mixing bowl, a rolling pin, a biscuit cutter and a baking tray, and you are away and cooking for your dog!

It is possible to purchase fancy biscuit cutters in the shapes of dog bones, kennels and many breeds of dogs. Along with Christmas, Valentine, Easter and birthday shapes, you can make your own celebration treats for your dogs and also use them as presents and fundraisers. I have included information in the appendices at the end of the book of where I've bought equipment that helped when baking for my dogs.

I love to experiment when cooking so be like me and add to the recipes. Herbs and spices and different vegetables that you have in your store cupboard can all be played with to find alternatives to the basic recipes provided. Chapter 12 details foods that are dangerous for dogs and that should not be fed to them – please contact me if you discover any more (*paddipaws@aol.com*).

Obesity in Dogs

Obesity is on the rise and sadly this includes our canine chums. With a pair of appealing eyes staring up at you it is far too easy to feed a little more to your dog. Be sensible – obesity in animals is increasingly common. Never follow the guidelines printed on dog food packets as to the 'ideal weight' for your pet; individual dogs can put on and lose weight at different rates.

No two dogs are the same. I have two litter brothers and, if I were to feed them identical meals, Buster the larger-framed boy would thrive whereas Nelson would lose weight. The reason is that Nelson is full of nervous energy. As a herding breed he is always on the go following the other dogs and never rests until he has them all in his sight and knows they are close by. Buster, on the other hand, is a big cuddly dog who is happy to sit by our sides and have his chest tickled. This shows that we have to know our pets and understand what they need to fuel their bodies. Another of our dogs, Molly, is a smaller Old English Sheepdog and never gained weight. After two operations and an illness her body has changed and if I am not careful she puts weight on, something I've never had a problem with in the past with my sheepdogs.

You need to get to know your dog's body and how it is structured. We are often told to look for lumps and bumps whilst bathing and grooming our pets, so at the same time feel their ribs and spine. Are they very prominent? Are they covered so well with a fat body that you have trouble feeling the bones? It's an age old guideline that works well for us today: feel the body of your dog and if you are not happy with what you feel then either increase his food intake or decrease it and exercise him more.

Special Diets

Chapter 10 includes advice on special diets. I give recipes for watching a dog's weight which seems to be as big a problem in pets today as it is with children and adults. There is a fashion these days to resort to raw or even vegetarian diets for dogs, but if we are not careful any diet can cause our pets to gain weight. Even weight-watching recipes can add weight if too much is fed to an animal.

Always take advice from your dog's breeder as they will have years of experience. (This is assuming you purchased your puppy from a reliable breeder – another book subject completely.) But if the breeder simply threw a sack of complete food in with the puppy sale without helpful guidance and a firm promise of free back-up for the life of the dog, then ignore their advice. Similarly, a vet's advice on feeding should be taken with a pinch of salt as so many these days work on commission from pet food manufacturers and will try to sell you the most expensive food on the market.

When to Feed
As the owner of a large breed, I am aware of bloat (gastric torsion) and have seen the disastrous and fatal effects on a much loved pet that was not treated correctly by a veterinary hospital. By feeding several meals each day rather than one you avoid overfilling the dog's stomach, which can be a possible factor in inducing bloat. Apart from medical reasons, a dog that eats when the family have their meals will not pester for food at the dining table and will know that his meals are served at regular times.

Changing a Dog's Diet
I recall meeting a lady while showing my dogs who was obsessed with different dog foods. At each show she would ask owners what they fed their dogs. Championship dog shows have a large array of pet food trade stands and she would always be seen asking their advice. This usually is a good thing, as we need to keep abreast of what is good for our dogs. However this lady bought the food and changed her dog's diet every few weeks, which had an effect on the condition and health of her animal. Her other obsession was her dog's health as he was either off his food or rather loose in the nether regions. She was so often at the vet that she must have had a consulting room named after her. She would never listen to knowledgeable dog people who told her it was the changes in her dog's diet that caused the problems.

No, instead she demanded skin tests and other expensive investigations on the poor dog until she found out that it was allergic to palm trees! No doubt she never told the vet that she changed the dog's food every other week as one would hope he or she would have advised her on the errors of her ways.

Any human has a reaction if they suddenly eat food that is alien to their previous diet. A new diet should be introduced gradually over two or three weeks so that any reactions can be monitored and adjusted accordingly. This is simply common sense for any pet owner.

You would have to search hard to find salt as an ingredient in my recipes included in this book. Instead I have used herbs and other flavourings such as stock cubes and garlic granules. The quantities given will not harm your dog's digestion or health.

Treats and Celebrations

There's nothing better than a party or a family event that involves food – why should our dogs be left out? Chapter 5 provides recipes for party and celebration food that can be eaten by dogs. One thing I ask is that you do not over indulge your pet. Never give them a normal day's feed on top of party food. Cutting back on their daily meals so they can have a slice of their doggy birthday cake will not hurt as long as it's not too often. The same goes for dog biscuits and other treats. Use them as part of the daily food quota or you will soon have a tubby dog. Moderation is the word to remember when treating your dog.

Training Aids

The majority of dogs will do anything for food, so a little titbit as a reward should work wonders when training a puppy. Praise and food can soon be replaced by just praise – there is no need to use food as a reward for the length of a dog's life.

My pet hate in the dog-showing world are the breeds that use bait in the show ring. Not only does the smell of food upset other dogs and put them off the job at hand, but the residue left in the grass is a nuisance for the next exhibitors using the ring. Anyone who has tried to keep a dog's nose off the ground when he has smelt sausage, cheese or liver will sympathise with this predicament. There is no need for food in the show ring. It just proves that the handler needs a crutch to fall back on when they cannot control their exhibit. Hopefully one day someone at the Kennel Club will introduce another little rule banning this annoying habit.

I hope that you enjoy cooking for your dogs. Involve your children and introduce them to the importance of canine food while they learn about grooming and training. Above all, love your dog every hour of the day as they leave us far too soon.

Biscuits and Everyday Treats

Get into the habit of baking your dog's biscuits and treats and you will soon see how much money you are saving. Not only that but you will have fresher, tastier food that your dog will enjoy. A large, plastic, airtight container or even an empty biscuit tin will serve to keep his tasty treats to hand and ready to eat. These recipes will be much healthier and better for his health than sharing one of your own sugar-laden biscuits at tea time.

These biscuits should be given as a treat and not as a meal replacement. If you are over generous when your dog looks at you with his large brown eyes, why not make smaller sized biscuits so he thinks he is getting more and you are in control?

There are many types of biscuit cutters on the market. We all have basic round and square cutters in our kitchen utensils drawer but why not try some of the specially designed cutters for dogs? Different breeds and dog-related shapes such as bones, cats and kennels are obtainable from cake supply shops and eBay.

Remember that different sized dogs need different sized biscuits!

Marmite Munchies

As the adverts say, your dog will either love them or hate them!

INGREDIENTS

3 mugs wholemeal flour

1 mug bulgur wheat

½ mug polenta

2 tbsp Marmite

1 mug warm water

TO MAKE

- ➤ Preheat the oven to 220°C/Gas Mark 7.
- ➤ Combine the dry ingredients in a large bowl.
- ➤ Melt the Marmite into the warm water and stir until dissolved.
- ➤ Gradually combine the Marmite mix with the dry ingredients until you have a stiff dough.
- ➤ Turn the dough out onto a floured board and knead well.
- ➤ With a floured rolling pin, roll out to a thickness of ½ cm.
- ➤ Using bone-shaped biscuit cutters, cut out the biscuits and place on a non-stick baking tray.
- ➤ Cook in the middle of the oven until the biscuits are brown and crunchy.
- ➤ Leave to cool and store in an airtight container, although they will not last long.

Flaxseed Straws

INGREDIENTS

500g plain flour	2 tbsp garlic granules
1 tsp salt	½ mug flaxseeds
250g lard	Cold water

TO MAKE

➤ Preheat the oven to 220°C/Gas Mark 7.

➤ Put the flour into a large bowl and stir in the salt.

➤ Cube the lard and add to the flour. Using your fingers, blend in the fat until the mix resembles very fine breadcrumbs.

➤ Add the garlic granules and flaxseeds and mix well.

➤ Add enough cold water to form a stiff dough.

➤ Turn the dough out onto a floured board and knead well to remove any air pockets.

➤ Roll out to a thickness of ½ cm. Using a sharp knife, cut the dough into strips of approximately ½ by 15 cm.

➤ Place onto a greased baking tray and pierce each straw several times with a fork to prevent them from rising too much.

➤ Bake in the middle of the oven and check after 15 min. The straws should be golden brown and crispy.

➤ Turn out onto a cooling tray and store in an airtight container when completely cold.

Note: You may find this recipe much easier to prepare in a food processor but do not over mix once the flaxseeds have been added.

Cheesey Twists

Dogs just love the flavour of cheese and it's one of the foods they will eat even when they are poorly.

INGREDIENTS

500g plain flour
1 tsp salt
1 tsp mustard powder

250g lard
250g strong flavoured cheese
Cold water

TO MAKE

➤ Preheat oven to 220°C/Gas Mark 7.

➤ Put the flour into a large bowl and stir in the salt and mustard powder.

➤ Cube the lard and add to the flour. Using your fingers, blend in the fat until the mix resembles very fine breadcrumbs.

➤ Finely grate the cheese and add to the dry mix stirring well.

➤ Add enough cold water to form a stiff dough.

➤ Turn the dough out onto a floured board and knead well to remove any air pockets.

➤ Roll out to a ½ cm thickness. Using a sharp knife, cut the dough into strips of approximately ½ by 15 cm.

➤ Place onto a greased baking tray and pierce each strip several times with a fork to prevent them from rising too much. Twist each strip twice into a spiral.

➤ Bake in the middle of the oven and check after 15 min. The twists should be golden brown and crispy.

➤ Turn out onto a cooling tray and store in an airtight container when completely cold.

Garlic Kisses

INGREDIENTS

500g plain flour
1 tsp salt
2 tbsp garlic granules

250g lard
Cold water

TO MAKE

➤ Preheat oven to 220°C/Gas Mark 7.
➤ Put the flour into a large bowl and stir in the salt and garlic granules.
➤ Cube the lard and add to the flour. Using your fingers, blend in the fat until the mix resembles very fine breadcrumbs.
➤ Add enough water to make a stiff dough.
➤ Turn the dough out onto a floured board and knead well to remove any air pockets.
➤ Roll out to a ½ cm thickness. Using a sharp knife, cut the dough into strips of approximately ½ by 15 cm.
➤ Pierce each strip several times with a fork to prevent them from rising too much.
➤ Cross each end of the strip over and carefully tie in a half-knot.
➤ Place onto a greased baking tray.
➤ Bake in the middle of the oven and check after 15 min. They should be golden brown and crispy. Check that the knotted part is cooked thoroughly.
➤ Turn out onto a cooling tray and sprinkle over a little more of the garlic granules.
➤ When cold, store in an airtight container.

Quick Doggy Donuts

This doggy favourite is quick and easy to prepare in the microwave.

INGREDIENTS

2 eggs

½ mug chicken stock

2 mugs wholegrain flour

½ mug porridge oats

1 cube chicken stock

1 round biscuit cutter

1 small biscuit cutter or an apple corer with a round end

TO MAKE

➤ Whisk the eggs and blend in the cold chicken stock.

➤ Gradually add the flour and the porridge oats until you have a firm dough.

➤ Turn onto a floured surface and roll out to a thickness of 1 ½ cm.

➤ Using the biscuit cutter, cut as many large round shapes as possible. Using the smaller cutter or corer, cut out a small round in the middle of every large round.

➤ Crush the stock cube and sprinkle a little on every donut.

➤ Arrange as many as you can onto a flat plate and place in the microwave. Cook for 5 min on high power; less if you have a higher powered oven. Increase the cooking time if a harder biscuit is required.

➤ Carefully remove from the oven and place on a cooling rack. Do not serve until they are cold.

➤ They will keep for three days in an airtight container.

Molasses Munchies

INGREDIENTS

3 mugs wholemeal flour

½ mug wheat germ

½ mug chopped almonds

1 tsp salt

½ mug softened margarine

½ mug softened margarine

1 mug molasses

Assortment of biscuit cutters

TO MAKE

➤ Preheat oven to 200°C/Gas Mark 6.

➤ Put the flour, wheat germ, almonds and salt into a large bowl and mix together.

➤ Using your fingers, crumble the margarine into the flour mixture until it resembles fine breadcrumbs.

➤ Beat the eggs and add to the flour mixture along with the molasses until you have a firm dough. If the dough is too soft add a little more flour; if dry add a little water.

➤ Turn the dough out onto a floured surface and roll out to a thickness of 1 ½ cm.

➤ Using the biscuit cutters, cut out desired shapes and place on a greased baking tray.

➤ Bake for 20 min or until the biscuits are browned.

➤ Leave on a cooling rack until completely cold before serving to the waiting hounds or storing in an airtight container.

Note: Molasses can be found in all good cookery stores as well as health food stores such as Holland and Barrett.

Carrot Crunchies

This non-meat crunchy biscuit is ideal for owners who prefer a vegetarian diet for their dogs.

INGREDIENTS

2 mugs plain flour

½ mug dried milk powder

6 carrots

5 Weetabix

2 tbsp vegetable oil

2 eggs, beaten

2 cubes vegetable stock

½ mug warm water

TO MAKE

➤ Preheat the oven to 220°C/Gas Mark 7.

➤ Put the plain flour and dried milk powder into a large mixing bowl. Mix together well.

➤ Finely grate the carrots and crumble 4 Weetabix. Add both to the bowl and stir.

➤ Add the vegetable oil and one of the beaten eggs.

➤ Dissolve the stock cubes into the water and gradually add to the mix until you have a stiff dough.

➤ Turn the dough out onto a floured surface and roll to approximately 1 cm thick.

➤ Using a round cutter, roughly mark the biscuits and carefully pull each one from the rolled-out dough. The grated carrot will give a rough appearance to the edges of each carrot crunchie rather like the expensive 'homemade' biscuits one sees in high-class bakeries.

➤ Brush the top of each crunchie with the second beaten egg and sprinkle more of the crumbled Weetabix on top.

➤ Place on a greased baking tray in the centre of the oven for 20 min or until the carrot crunchies are cooked through and crispy.

Note: You may need to adjust the liquid content when making the dough. If the mix is too sticky add more flour.

Molly's Milk Bone Biccies

Our youngest dog, Molly, has a tendency to put on weight. There's no denying the fact that she is a coach potato in the form of an Old English Sheepdog. I bake these tasty biscuits and use the smallest bone shaped cutters I have so that she has her treat but as a diet-sized treat.

INGREDIENTS

½ mug beef suet

1 mug hot water

½ mug dried milk powder

4 mugs malted wheat grain flour

2 eggs

1 egg white

TO MAKE

➤ Preheat the oven to 180°C/Gas Mark 4.

➤ Into a large mixing bowl put the beef suet and pour the hot water on top. Stir until the suet has melted. Allow to cool slightly before adding the rest of the ingredients as follows.

➤ Add the milk powder, stirring all the time, followed by half of the flour.

➤ Beat the two eggs and add to the mixture.

➤ Add the rest of the flour to form a firm dough. You may need to add a little water if the mixture is too stiff.

➤ Turn the dough out onto a floured surface and roll to a depth of just over 1 cm.

➤ Using a bone-shaped cutter, cut the milk biscuit shapes and place on a lightly greased baking tray.

➤ Place onto the centre rack of your oven and bake for 50 min or until hard.

➤ Remove from the oven and transfer to a cooling tray. Immediately brush each biscuit with egg white to give them a shiny gloss.

➤ When cool, store in an airtight container.

Note: The smaller the biscuit, the less baking time required.

Buster's Bacon Bites

Our Buster is a big cuddly dog who loves nothing more than sharing our food. He is particularly interested when bacon is being fried, so this recipe was designed to suit him. He did appreciate the gesture!

INGREDIENTS

250g pack bacon pieces	5 eggs
4 mugs organic wholemeal flour	1 mug milk

TO MAKE

- ➤ Preheat the oven to 200°C/Gas Mark 6.
- ➤ Chop the bacon into small pieces and fry in a large non-stick frying pan until crispy. When cool, tip the bacon and residue of fat into a large mixing bowl.
- ➤ Add the flour and stir.
- ➤ Beat the eggs and add to the bacon and flour mix.
- ➤ Gradually add the milk and stir well to break down any lumps in the flour. You should have a dropping consistency.
- ➤ Drop heaped spoonfuls onto a greased baking tray and place in the oven to cook.
- ➤ If you turn off the oven when cooking has finished, these bacon bites will harden overnight.
- ➤ Alternatively you could cook them on top of the cooker on a griddle, but they are best served hard and crispy.

Note: This is an ideal recipe for the cheaply priced bacon scraps found in most supermarkets.

Nutty Banana Biccies

This recipe is a great way to use up leftover nuts and soft bananas.

INGREDIENTS

4 mugs organic plain flour	2 eggs
½ mug of chopped nuts	1 tsp banana essence
4 bananas	A little milk

TO MAKE

- ➤ Preheat the oven to 200°C/Gas Mark 6.
- ➤ Place the flour and chopped nuts into a large mixing bowl.
- ➤ Mash the banana with a fork and add to the mixture.
- ➤ Whisk the eggs and stir into the flour mixture along with the banana essence.
- ➤ Use the milk to mix to a stiff dough.
- ➤ Turn the dough out onto a floured surface and knead well by hand.
- ➤ Pull off pieces of the dough and shape into long tubes. Slightly flatten these tubes and place them onto a greased baking tray, bending each into a curve rather like a banana.
- ➤ Bake in the oven for about 15 min until the nutty banana biccies are golden brown.
- ➤ These biccies can be stored in an airtight container.

Easy Peasey Cheesey Bics

This is such an easy recipe to prepare, why not let your children help you bake the biscuits?

INGREDIENTS

100g cheese	1 tsp garlic salt
2 mugs plain flour	Water
100g margarine	

TO MAKE

- ➤ Preheat the oven to 220°C/Gas Mark 7.
- ➤ Grate the cheese into a large mixing bowl.
- ➤ Add the flour and margarine and blend well together using your fingers.
- ➤ Add the garlic salt and stir well.
- ➤ Add enough water to form a dough.
- ➤ Cover with cling film and leave for 2 hours in the fridge to chill.
- ➤ Place the dough onto a floured surface and roll out to a thickness of about 1 cm or thinner for small dogs.
- ➤ Cut into shapes and place on a non-stick baking tray in the top of the oven.
- ➤ Bake for 15 min or until the biscuits have browned.
- ➤ Turn out onto a cooling rack and allow to cool before storing in an airtight container.

Chicken, Apple and Cinnamon Cakes

This does sound like a strange combination but my dogs just love these cakes! They look like rock cakes.

INGREDIENTS

1 cooking apple	4 tbsp vegetable oil
2 mugs self-raising flour	2 tbsp cinnamon
1 cube chicken stock	1 mug water
1 mug porridge oats	

TO MAKE

➤ Preheat the oven to 200°C/Gas Mark 6.

➤ Peel the apple and remove the core. Roughly chop into pieces of around 1½ cm.

➤ Combine all the dry ingredients and the apple in a large mixing bowl, remembering to crumble the chicken stock cube.

➤ Add the water gradually until you have a firm mix that resembles a rock cake mixture.

➤ Place dessertspoon-sized drops of the mixture onto a non-stick baking tray and bake in the middle of the oven until they are golden brown.

➤ Allow to cool before storing in an airtight container.

Note: Chopped or grated carrot also works well in this recipe.

Honey and Apple Cookies

Tasty and easy to make!

INGREDIENTS

1 cooking apple

4 tbsp runny honey

½ mug water

1 tsp cinnamon

1 mug porridge oats

1 mug wholemeal flour

½ mug bran flakes

TO MAKE

- ➤ Preheat the oven to 200°C/Gas Mark 6.
- ➤ Peel and roughly chop the apple.
- ➤ Put the apple along with the honey, water, cinnamon and porridge oats into a mixing bowl. Mix well.
- ➤ Gradually stir in the flour and bran flakes until you have a stiff dough. Use a little more water if needed.
- ➤ Drop spoonfuls of the mixture onto a non-stick baking tray. The size depends on the size of your dog.
- ➤ Using the back of a spoon, slightly flatten each cookie.
- ➤ Bake in the centre of the oven for about 30 min, turning them once halfway through the baking time.
- ➤ Allow to cool thoroughly before treating your dog.
- ➤ These cookies can be stored in an airtight container.

Vegetable Cookies

These are an interesting twist on the sweet cookies favoured by humans. They are full of flavour and smell divine.

INGREDIENTS

3 carrots	1 mug wholemeal flour
2 mugs brown rice	2 tbsp gravy granules
2 mugs porridge oats	2 tbsp molasses
½ mug low fat milk	4 tbsp apple sauce
1 mug frozen spinach	1 tbsp vegetable oil

TO MAKE

➤ Preheat the oven to 200°C/Gas Mark 6.

➤ Wash and finely chop the carrots.

➤ Put all ingredients into a large mixing bowl and stir well to form a firm mix that can drop from a spoon. Add a little water if the mixture is too stiff.

➤ Drop spoonfuls of the mixture onto a non-stick baking tray and gently press each one flat with a spoon.

➤ Place in the middle of the oven and bake for 15–20 min or until golden brown. Turn once during the cooking time so both sides are crispy.

➤ Place on a cooling rack until cold.

➤ They can be stored in an airtight container.

Nutty Sesame Circles

An interesting recipe and one that humans would enjoy as well!

INGREDIENTS

2 mugs plain flour

½ mug brown sugar

½ mug runny honey

½ mug sesame seeds

Rind of 2 lemons

100g margarine

½ mug walnuts, chopped

1 tsp vanilla extract

TO MAKE

➤ Place all ingredients into a large mixing bowl and combine well to form a dough. Add a little milk if needed.

➤ Turn the dough onto a floured surface and knead before splitting into four parts.

➤ Roll each part into a log shape about the size of a Swiss roll. Cover in cling film and place in the fridge for several hours until well chilled.

➤ Preheat the oven to 220°C/Gas Mark 7.

➤ Remove the dough rolls from the fridge and slice each into small circles.

➤ Place onto a non-stick baking tray and bake for approximately 15 min.

➤ Place onto a cooling rack until cold and store in an airtight container.

Soft Beef Cookies

These easy-to-make cookies are ideal for older dogs who find it hard to chew on crunchier biscuits.

INGREDIENTS

3 jars beef baby food

½ mug dried milk powder

1 mug wholemeal flour

TO MAKE

➤ Preheat the oven to 220°C/Gas Mark 7.

- ➤ Put all the ingredients into a mixing bowl and combine well.
- ➤ Take small portions of the mix and roll into small balls.
- ➤ Place onto a non-stick baking tray and flatten slightly with the back of a spoon.
- ➤ Cook for 15 min or until brown.
- ➤ Leave to cool on a wire cooling rack.
- ➤ To store, freeze on a flat tray and then divide between portion-sized bags.

Beef-flavoured Biccies

Potato flour is the base for this beefy treat and can be purchased in most health food stores.

INGREDIENTS

2 mugs potato flour

4 tbsp chopped parsley

½ mug vegetable oil

3 cubes beef stock

1 ½ mugs warm water

TO MAKE

- ➤ Preheat the oven to 200°C/Gas Mark 6.
- ➤ Place the potato flour, parsley and vegetable oil into a bowl and mix well.
- ➤ Dissolve the beef stock cubes in the warm water and gradually add to the mix until a stiff dough has formed.
- ➤ Turn the dough out onto a floured surface and roll out to a thickness of 1 ½ cm.
- ➤ Cut into shapes to suit the size of your dog.
- ➤ Place onto a non-stick baking tray and bake for 30 min until the biscuits are brown and crispy.
- ➤ Place onto a wire rack until completely cool.
- ➤ Store in an airtight container until needed.

Cook and Freeze

If you are preparing food for the family's freezer, why not cook for your dog as well. Defrosting a bag of wholesome fresh food is so much better for your dog than a scoop of highly coloured kibble, isn't it?

Most canine recipes do not take long to prepare and can be cooked in a slow cooker or in the bottom of the oven whilst you are preparing a family meal. A pressure cooker can also turn out delicious meals, as can careful use of a microwave oven.

Once food is cool, pack into plastic storage containers that are approved for the freezer or in strong durable bags. Label and date each container with details of the contents so they are easily identified.

Rotate the food in your freezer, making sure the oldest food is used first. I like to keep my food no longer than 3 months although many foods can be stored much longer than this if freezer guidelines are to be believed.

Take your dog's meal from the freezer and defrost slowly in the fridge, overnight if possible. It is possible to defrost food in a microwave but follow guidelines carefully so as not to cook and burn the food.

Some stews and meat products can be tipped from frozen into a casserole dish, covered with a lid or foil and heated through in the oven. If you try this, remember to check that the food is heated through properly but not so hot that your dog burns his mouth.

Being able to dip into your freezer for a home-cooked meal for your dog is very satisfying.

Paw Licking Meatballs

This is a lovely recipe to freeze and keep ready for when you do not have time to prepare a freshly made meal for your dog. The balls are best frozen on a tray in the freezer and then bagged in individual portions to save them sticking together. Use your own kibble recipe to make this a truly homemade meal for your hungry dog.

INGREDIENTS

2 mugs homemade kibble	2 cloves of garlic
500g minced chicken	2 eggs
½ mug vegetable oil	4 tbsp runny honey
Handful of parsley, chopped	Water if needed

TO MAKE

➤ Place the kibble into a polythene bag and break it into small pieces by bashing with a rolling pin. The finer the better as it will mix well with the raw meat. Tip into a large bowl.

➤ Stir in the minced chicken meat. Add the chopped parsley.

➤ Finely chop the garlic and add to the mix.

➤ Beat the eggs and add to the bowl along with the runny honey.

➤ Mix well together to form a hamburger consistency. If the mix is too dry, gradually add small amounts of water.

➤ Using floured hands, take small amounts of the meatball mixture and roll into evenly sized balls. The size of the ball depends on the size of your dog.

➤ At this point the meatballs can be frozen.

TO COOK

Place the required amount of meatballs into a pan of stock and simmer for 20 min or until cooked through. Alternatively they can be baked in the oven and served with leftover gravy from the family meal.

Note: This is an ideal way to use up all those small pieces of kibble at the bottom of the food sack.

Winter Warming Beef Stew

This is an easy meal to make that can be frozen in batches, thawed and served to a hungry dog. Use shin or stewing beef. The cheaper cuts of beef will cook well if simmered or casseroled for several hours.

INGREDIENTS

3 tbsp vegetable oil	6 large potatoes
1 kg stewing beef	3 cloves of garlic, crushed
10 mugs chicken stock	2 mugs pearl barley
(can be made from stock cubes)	1 mug brown rice
6 carrots	Gravy granules to thicken

TO MAKE

➤ Heat the vegetable oil in a large stew pan.

➤ Dice the stewing beef into dog mouth-sized pieces and brown.

➤ Add the stock, bring to the boil and lower heat to simmer.

➤ Wash, peel and chop the carrots and potato into large chunks and add to the pan along with the crushed garlic. Any seasonal root vegetable may be used for this recipe.

➤ Simmer for 2 hours on a low heat before adding the pearl barley and brown rice. Continue simmering until the meat is really tender and almost falling apart. Stir well to avoid the rice sticking to the bottom of the pan.

➤ Thicken with the gravy granules and leave to cool.

➤ Divide into portions and freeze in containers ready for use.

Note: Many supermarkets sell 'soup and stew mixes' which are ideal for dog recipes. I also like to use up meat from my freezer or buy meat that has been reduced in price as it is near to its sell by date. Frozen vegetable packs are also good value when cooking this stew.

For Aga owners, this recipe can sit in the oven for hours on a low heat. If you use a slow cooker the recipe can be adapted for this useful cooking aid.

Fish Stew

Any pieces of fish that are on offer in your local supermarket can be used in this recipe.

INGREDIENTS

1 kg fish pieces e.g. cod, coley,
   mackerel, herring
1 small tub chicken livers
1 mug fish stock made from a stock cube
1 mug chopped raw spinach

½ mug sliced green beans
½ mug sweetcorn
2 large potatoes, peeled and cubed
1 mug long grain rice
2 tbsp cod liver oil

TO MAKE

➤ Preheat the oven to 180°C/Gas Mark 4.
➤ Chop the fish into doggy bite-sized pieces and place into a large baking tin.
➤ Chop the chicken liver and add with the vegetables to the baking tin. Cover with the fish stock.
➤ Place into the middle of the preheated oven and cook for 40 min.
➤ Meanwhile, cook the rice in boiling water and then drain.
➤ When the fish and vegetable mix is cooked, add the rice. This should soak up the excess liquid in the baking tin.
➤ Finally add the cod liver oil.
➤ This dish can be served when cooled or bagged into portions and frozen for future use.

Hayley's Hearts

Lamb hearts are a good source of nutrition and dogs love them. Our Hayley loved this meal and it was a favourite extra meal when she was expecting her litter of puppies. The recipe must have been good as she had nine healthy sheepdog babies, many of whom reached over 14 years of age.

INGREDIENTS

1 lamb heart

1 tbsp vegetable oil

1 potato

1 large carrot

1 cube lamb stock

2 mugs water

1 tbsp gravy granules

TO MAKE

➤ Cut the lamb heart into 2 ½ cm cubes.

➤ Heat the vegetable oil in a heavy base pan and add the cubed lamb heart. Cook gently until browned on all sides.

➤ Peel and dice the potato and carrot and add to the pan along with the stock cube and water.

➤ Bring to the boil and leave to simmer for 1 hour or until the meat is tender.

➤ Add the gravy granules to thicken and remove from the heat to cool.

➤ Serve with homemade mixer biscuit. Delicious!

➤ This recipe can be frozen in small portions ready to reheat when desired.

Munchy Pork Lunch

Pork belly strips are economical and taste good. Most dogs will find them appealing when they are prepared in this delicious way.

INGREDIENTS

2 thick pork belly strips	1 parsnip
1 tbsp vegetable oil	½ mug hot water
1 potato	1 cube vegetable stock
1 carrot	1 large eating apple

TO MAKE

➤ Preheat the oven to 200°C/Gas Mark 6.

➤ Cut each pork belly strip into 2 lengths of ½ cm.

➤ Heat the vegetable oil in a frying pan and add the pork. Cook long enough to seal the meat.

➤ Meanwhile, peel the potato, carrot and parsnip and cut into strips 5 cm in length, rather like chips. Add these to the pan and cook for 5 min.

➤ Add the water and stock cube and bring to the boil. Leave to simmer for 20 min.

➤ Transfer to a heatproof casserole dish.

➤ Peel and dice the apple and add to the meat and vegetables.

➤ Cover the casserole dish and place in the middle of the preheated oven for 50 min. At this point the gravy can be thickened if preferred.

➤ Leave to cool, then serve with homemade mixer biscuit. This is another recipe that freezes well.

Note: If you are watching your dog's weight, then serve with extra root vegetables.

Nellie Rolls

Whenever we eat sausage rolls our dogs line up for a taste. I devised this recipe for 'our Nellie', who loves human food rather than his own. As the pastry in this recipe is so thin, your dog can enjoy these rolls without putting on excess weight.

INGREDIENTS

1 mug white rice

250g lean minced beef

1 tsp garlic granules

3 eggs

1 pack readymade short crust pastry

Flour for rolling

TO MAKE

➤ Preheat the oven to 200°C/Gas Mark 6.

➤ Place the rice into a pan of salted boiling water and cook until very soft. Drain and cool.

➤ Put the minced beef, cold rice and garlic granules into a mixing bowl.

➤ Mix well until all ingredients are combined.

➤ Beat the eggs well and add ¾ to the mixture, retaining the rest to glaze the Nellie Rolls.

➤ Turn out the mix onto a floured board and using floured hands shape the mix into long chipolata-sized lengths.

➤ Roll out the pastry until it is very thin but has not split. Cut into 7½ cm widths. Place the sausage mix onto the pastry and roll the sides over to cover it, using beaten egg to seal any edges.

➤ Cut into 2½ cm pieces and brush with the beaten egg.

➤ Place onto a non-stick baking tray and cook in the centre of the oven until brown and glistening.

➤ Remove and place onto a cooling tray covered in kitchen paper. This will soak up any excess oil.

➤ These rolls freeze very well.

Note: I make the filling in my food processor as a rule, as it combines the rice and minced beef effectively.

Frozen Rice Balls

These rice balls are easy to make and they freeze really well. Open freezing them enables you to pack them easily and remove them individually when needed. This recipe makes a large batch but it can be adjusted to suit your dog and your freezer capacity.

INGREDIENTS

10 chicken thighs	3 broccoli stems
Water	3 large carrots
3 cubes chicken stock	1 clove of garlic
5 mugs organic rice	1 mug frozen runner beans

TO MAKE

➤ Place the chicken thighs into a large pan with enough water to cover. Crumble the stock cubes into the pan and simmer until the chicken is well cooked and falling from the bone.

➤ Drain and keep the stock.

➤ Remove the bones from the chicken and chop the meat finely.

➤ Add the rice to the stock and cook until tender. Drain and leave to cool.

➤ At the same time, wash and prepare the vegetables. Chop into small pieces and place into a pan of water. Bring to the boil and simmer until tender. When cooked drain and allow to cool.

➤ Place all the ingredients into a large mixing bowl and combine well.

➤ Dampen your hands and take small amounts of the mix. Roll it to form balls suitable for the size of your dog. Place each ball onto a tray and cover with cling film.

➤ Freeze overnight before placing into plastic bags or a container for storage.

Note: These balls can either be defrosted and served to your dog or dropped into a pan of stock to warm through.

Liver and Bacon Stew

Dogs just love liver and I use it quite often for training treats and snacks. Stewed in a slow cooker or low temperature oven, the liver falls apart so older dogs do not even need to chew too much.

INGREDIENTS

1 tbsp butter
6 rashers streaky bacon
500 g pig liver
1 tbsp garlic granules

1 cube beef stock
2 mugs water
3 tsp corn flour

TO MAKE

➤ Heat the butter in a heavy-based frying pan.
➤ Chop the bacon into 2½ cm squares and add to the pan. Fry until just cooked.
➤ Add the liver pieces and cook for a few minutes on each side. Remove the liver and slice thinly before cutting into 2½ cm squares. Return to the frying pan along with any blood from the packet.
➤ Add the garlic granules, stock cube and water. Bring up to heat.
➤ Carefully add the ingredients into a slow cooker and set to cook for the day.
➤ Before serving, add the corn flour to a little water and mix to a smooth paste. Pour into the stew and stir until thickened.
➤ Remove the stew and allow to cool before serving or decanting into containers for the freezer.

Lovely Lamb

Cheaper cuts of meat that are slow cooked are tender enough even for older dogs.

INGREDIENTS

2 breasts of lamb	2 cubes lamb stock
1 tbsp vegetable oil	1 tsp dried rosemary
½ small onion	3 mugs water
1 clove of garlic	3 tbsp corn flour
6 carrots	1 mug frozen peas

TO MAKE

➤ Preheat the oven to 180°C/Gas Mark 4 or use a slow cooker.

➤ Cut the lamb into evenly sized chunks between the bones.

➤ Heat the oil and add the lamb, sealing all sides of the meat.

➤ Finely chop the onion and the garlic and add to the pan. Stir until the onion is soft but not brown.

➤ Wash and slice the carrot into thick chunks. Add to the pan with the meat.

➤ Add the stock cubes, rosemary and water and bring to a simmer.

➤ Transfer to an ovenproof dish, or the slow cooker, and leave to cook slowly in the oven for 3 hours, or longer.

➤ Remove from the oven and pull the bones from the meat. They should just fall away.

➤ Mix the corn flour with a little water and stir until you have a lump-free paste. Stir into the casserole until it thickens.

➤ Add the frozen peas.

➤ Allow to cool and then divide into dog-sized portions. Store in freezer bags and label.

Christmas Turkey Dinner

This is an ideal meal to have ready in the freezer so that your dog can enjoy his Christmas meal with you. Add vegetables from the table and readymade mixer biscuit.

INGREDIENTS

1 tbsp vegetable oil	½ mug sage and onion stuffing mix
500g turkey mince	2 tbsp turkey-flavoured gravy granules
1 cube chicken or turkey stock	4 slices streaky bacon
2 mugs water	12 pork cocktail sausages

TO MAKE

➤ Preheat the oven to 200°C/Gas Mark 6.

➤ Heat the oil in a deep saucepan. Add the turkey mince and cook for 10 min until slightly brown.

➤ Crumble in the stock cubes and add the water. Bring to the boil and then simmer for 30 min on a low heat.

➤ Remove from the heat and add the sage and onion mix. Add extra hot water if necessary as the mix should be thick but fluid. Add the gravy granules.

➤ Transfer to an ovenproof dish and place in the oven for 45 min.

➤ Meanwhile, cut each rasher of streaky bacon into three and wrap a piece around each cocktail sausage. Place under the grill on a low heat and cook until the bacon is brown. Remove and leave to cool.

➤ Remove the casserole from the oven and allow to cool.

➤ Place portions of the turkey meal into containers and divide the sausages between the meals.

➤ Freeze until needed.

Roast Vegetables and Chicken

This meal uses many ingredients that you would have in your freezer and vegetable store.

INGREDIENTS

3 tbsp olive oil

6 chicken thighs with the bones removed

2 large potatoes

1 red onion

2 large carrots

1 parsnip

10 baby sweetcorn

1 tbsp dried rosemary

1 tbsp garlic granules

1 mug hot water

1 tbsp chicken gravy granules or cornflour

TO MAKE

➤ Preheat the oven to 220°C/Gas Mark 7.

➤ In a frying pan heat a little of the oil and brown the chicken. Transfer to a deep baking tray.

➤ Wash the vegetables and chop into large pieces. Scatter them amongst the chicken pieces.

➤ Sprinkle the rosemary and garlic granules over the prepared dish, followed by the rest of the olive oil.

➤ Place in a hot oven for 45 min, taking care to turn the vegetables and chicken so they do not burn.

➤ Remove from the heat and allow to cool.

➤ Divide the food into dog-sized portions.

➤ Return the tray to the top of the cooker and add a mug of hot water to de-glaze the tray. Add gravy granules or corn flour to make a gravy. When cool, carefully tip a little into each container and then freeze.

Note: Foil containers with lids are ideal for this recipe.

Pork and Potatoes

With so many tasty ingredients, this recipe will tempt any dog to eat.

INGREDIENTS

100g diced pork	2 tsp ground ginger
3 tbsp corn flour	2 cubes vegetable stock
1 tbsp vegetable oil	1 mug water
1 clove of garlic	2 large potatoes
1 cooking apple	4 tbsp tomato paste

TO MAKE

➤ Coat the pork in the corn flour.

➤ Heat the oil in a pan and add the pork.

➤ Crush the garlic and peel, core and dice the apple. Add to the pan along with the ginger, stock cubes and water.

➤ Peel and dice the potato and add to the pan along with the tomato paste.

➤ Lower the heat and simmer for 1 hour.

➤ Remove and allow to cool before freezing.

Savoury Stir Fry

This is a slightly different way to serve meat and vegetables to your dog.

INGREDIENTS

1 mug brown rice

2 tbsp vegetable oil

200g stewing steak

1 clove of garlic

1 carrot

1 broccoli stem

1 mug white cabbage, chopped

2 tbsp light soy sauce

½ mug water

1 cube beef stock

TO MAKE

➤ Place the rice in boiling water and cook until just soft.

➤ Heat the oil in a wok or deep frying pan.

➤ Thinly slice the stewing steak and fry until cooked through.

➤ Crush the garlic, thinly slice the carrot and chop the broccoli before adding them to the mix.

➤ Add the white cabbage and fry for 5 min.

➤ Add the soy sauce, water and stock cube and simmer. Then add the cooked rice, allowing it to soak up the sauce.

➤ Remove from the heat and leave to cool.

➤ Divide into containers and when cold place in the freezer.

Chicken Meat Loaf

Meat loaf is so easy to make. Stored in the freezer in slices, it will defrost in no time.

INGREDIENTS

½ mug white long grain rice

1 mug homemade kibble or mixer biscuit

1 mug hot water

2 cubes chicken stock

2 eggs

300 g raw chicken mince

3 carrots

TO MAKE

➤ Preheat the oven to 200°C/Gas Mark 6.

➤ Cover the rice with boiling water and simmer until cooked. Remove from the heat and drain. Allow to cool before use.

➤ Place the kibble or mixer biscuit in a bowl and add the hot water and stock cubes.

➤ Beat the eggs and add to the mix along with the chicken mince. Stir well.

➤ Grate the carrot and add to the mixture along with the cooked rice.

➤ Pack the mixture into a loaf tin and place in the oven for 45 min.

➤ When cold, remove from the loaf tin and slice.

➤ Wrap each portion and freeze until needed.

Beefy Rice and Beans

This recipe is easy to make, so prepare a large batch and stock up for days when you don't feel like cooking.

INGREDIENTS

1 mug brown rice	1 small onion
1 tbsp vegetable oil	2 cloves of garlic
500g minced beef	2 cans baked beans in tomato sauce

TO MAKE

➤ Place the rice in a pan of boiling water and cook until soft. Drain.

➤ Heat the oil and add the minced beef.

➤ Chop the onion and garlic and add to the mince.

➤ Cook slowly until the minced beef is cooked through.

➤ Add the baked beans and rice and stir well.

➤ Remove from the heat and allow to cool.

➤ Divide into containers and freeze.

Daily Recipes

Quite often I will cook something for my dogs while preparing the family meal. It's very easy to peel a few more vegetables or add another casserole dish to the oven. It costs no more in fuel and the time spent in preparation is minimal.

When shopping for food, I will add another pound or so of meat to my shopping trolley. I like to use human-grade meat for my dogs as sometimes it is false economy to purchase animal-grade foodstuff. I do buy the cheaper priced, human-grade minced beef as the little extra fat can help body up a skinny dog and a small amount of fat adds taste.

Get into the habit of planning your family's menu for the week and add to the shopping list the items needed to cook for your dog. You will be surprised at how little it in fact costs to feed your dog with fresh, healthy food compared with costlier complete dog feeds. I've nothing against food made specifically for dogs – I do use it myself. But there is definitely a place for both home-cooked and convenience food for the family pets.

Quickie Dinner

When cooking the family meal with minced beef, why not cook for your dog at the same time?

INGREDIENTS

250g (or one small tray) of minced beef ½ mug frozen runner beans
1 large potato 1 cube beef stock
½ mug brown rice

TO MAKE

➤ Place the minced beef into a non-stick pan and cook until well browned.
➤ Wash the potato and cut into 2½ cm cubes. Put it with the rice into a pan of boiling water and simmer until cooked.
➤ Drain and add to the minced beef along with the runner beans and crumbled stock cube.
➤ Stir for 2 min or until the runner beans are cooked.
➤ Tip into a dog bowl and serve when cooled.

Note: This meal will serve one large dog so divide it into suitable portions for smaller dogs and refrigerate for the next day's meal.

Potatoes au Puppy

This is a quick nutritional meal that can be made at the same time as preparing the family supper. This recipe is not only good for adult dogs but for puppies as well.

INGREDIENTS

2 large potatoes	1 small tub cottage cheese
2 eggs	1 mug milk
1 mug carrots, grated	½ mug cheese, grated
½ mug frozen peas	

TO MAKE

➤ Preheat the oven to 200°C/Gas Mark 6.

➤ Wash and peel the potatoes. Slice them into 1½ cm pieces and cook in boiling water until soft.

➤ At the same time, place the eggs into a pan of boiling water and cook for 8 min. Then plunge the eggs into cold water to cool before removing the shells and slicing thinly.

➤ Grease a casserole dish and layer the potatoes, egg, vegetables and cottage cheese until they are all used, ending with a layer of potato.

➤ Pour the milk over the potato and top with the grated cheese.

➤ Place in the middle of the oven for approximately 30 min or until the cheese is golden brown.

➤ Remove and allow to cool thoroughly before serving to your dog.

Yummy Steamed Pudding

This pudding is best prepared using a food processor as the ingredients need to be finely chopped and mixed together to give an even texture to the end result. It's an ideal meal to cook for your pet while making a steamed pudding for the family.

INGREDIENTS

2 large carrots	250g (or one small tray) minced turkey
1 turnip	1 cube chicken stock
1 parsnip	½ mug vegetable suet
1 large potato	½ mug plain wholemeal flour
2 cloves of garlic	2 eggs, beaten

TO MAKE

➤ Wash the carrots, turnip, parsnip and potato. There is no need to peel the vegetables.

➤ Feed the vegetables and the garlic into the food processor and pulse until they resemble fine breadcrumbs.

➤ Add the minced turkey and crumbled stock cube and mix well together.

➤ Add the suet and flour followed by the 2 beaten eggs.

➤ Pack tightly into a greased pudding bowl and seal with greaseproof paper or foil.

➤ Place in a steamer and steam for 2 hours, checking that the water is topped up at all times.

➤ The pudding should be served when it has cooled. If you prefer, this recipe could make two smaller puddings.

Note: If you do not have a steamer, place an upturned saucer in a large pan and place the pudding bowl on top while cooking. Check the water level at all times.

Fried Fish and Rice

This is a great recipe for the dog as the ingredients can usually be found hiding in the freezer and store cupboard. Ensure all bones are removed from the fish. It's a rather tasty dish for the family as well!

INGREDIENTS

½ mug brown rice

1 fish fillet (cod, plaice or even salmon)

1 tbsp vegetable oil

1 carrot, finely chopped

½ mug white cabbage, chopped

1 celery stalk, finely chopped

1 egg, beaten

A matchbox-sized piece of cheese

TO MAKE

➤ Place the rice into boiled water and simmer until cooked. Drain and leave to cool.

➤ Steam the fish until it is cooked, leave to cool and break into evenly sized flakes.

➤ Heat the vegetable oil in a heavy-based frying pan and add the chopped vegetables. Stir fry until just cooked through.

➤ Add the cooked rice and stir until warmed through.

➤ Beat the egg and add to the pan, continuing to stir as the egg thickens.

➤ Carefully stir in the flaked fish.

➤ Crumble the cheese and scatter over the rice dish. Place under a hot grill for a few minutes until the cheese has browned.

➤ Carefully remove from the pan and place onto a plate to cool.

➤ Serve in slices or chopped up. Add more rice and vegetables if you are cooking for a larger dog.

Poochie Pasta

Making pasta is easy and so delicious. Why not make it for your favourite pet?

INGREDIENTS

250g or 1 small supermarket pack of liver (any type)

1 clove of garlic, crushed

3 eggs

3 mugs wholemeal flour

2 tbsp olive oil

TO MAKE

➤ Place the liver and garlic into a blender and puree to a smooth paste.

➤ Add the eggs and blend well together.

➤ Place the flour into a large bowl and add the liver mixture and the olive oil. Mix well and turn out onto a floured board.

➤ Knead the liver dough for a few minutes before wrapping in cling film and allow it to rest in the fridge for several hours.

➤ Then cut a piece from the dough and roll out thinly. Cut into shapes or strips.

➤ Bring a pan of water to the boil and place the pasta into the pan. Cook until al dente.

➤ Serve with fresh vegetables, cottage cheese or natural yoghurt for a tasty sauce.

Note: If you have garlic-flavoured olive oil in your store cupboard, this is an ideal substitute for raw garlic.

Corned Beef Patties

This easy-to-make recipe is ideal for picnics and while you are travelling. It packs well and is full of good things for your dog to eat.

INGREDIENTS

1 small tin corned beef

Variety of vegetables e.g. broccoli, cauliflower, sweetcorn, peas

6 eggs

1 large tub low fat cottage cheese

Small piece of cheddar cheese

TO MAKE

➤ Preheat the oven to 220°C/Gas Mark 7.

➤ Chop the corned beef into small cubes and put some in the bottom of each compartment of a non-stick bun tray.

➤ Chop the vegetables into small pieces and cook in a little water until they are slightly crispy. Drain and leave to cool.

➤ In a mixing bowl place the eggs and cottage cheese and beat well together.

➤ Divide the vegetables between each bun tray compartment and pour a little of the egg mixture into each.

➤ Grate the cheese and scatter over each pattie.

➤ Bake in the middle of the oven until cooked through. Test to see if cooked using a metal skewer.

➤ Turn out onto a cooling tray and pack into an airtight container if using as a picnic meal.

Carob Cake

We all know that dogs should not be given chocolate, but carob is a tasty alternative. A portion of this dish can be served to your dog along with his meat meal, but watch the portion size or your dog will gain weight. This recipe can be made in a food processor or mixer and is prepared in minutes.

INGREDIENTS

2 mugs wholemeal flour	3 eggs
1 mug milk	1 tsp vanilla flavouring
125g margarine (or approx. ½ a block)	1 small bar of carob

TO MAKE

➤ Preheat the oven to 190°C/Gas Mark 5.

➤ Place the flour, milk, margarine, eggs and vanilla into the food processor and mix until you have a smooth consistency.

➤ Melt the carob in a bowl over a pan of hot water. Add to the cake mix and pulse until well blended.

➤ Pour the mix into a loaf tin that has been greased and floured to prevent sticking.

➤ Place into the centre of the oven and bake for 50 min or until cooked through. Test with a skewer to check that the centre of the cake is cooked.

➤ Turn out onto a cooling tray and leave to cool fully before serving.

➤ This loaf can be decorated with cream cheese or more carob to turn it into a splendid celebration cake.

Scrambled Egg for Tiny Pups

Scrambled egg is ideal for young puppies when introducing them to solid food. By adding a twist to the usual recipe it can become a high protein, tasty meal for any dog.

INGREDIENTS

4 eggs	1 tbsp vegetable oil
Milk	Small portion of raw minced beef

TO MAKE

- ➤ Whisk the eggs with a small amount of milk.
- ➤ Add the oil to a non-stick pan and heat thoroughly.
- ➤ Add the egg mix and keep stirring to stop the egg sticking to the pan.
- ➤ As the egg thickens, add the raw minced beef in small ball-sized portions and heat until the meat is just cooked through.
- ➤ Allow to cool and serve to the hungry puppy.

Note: If you are introducing a young dog to meat for the first time, only give him small portions. Try feeding small pieces of the raw meat to give him the taste and he will soon be eating from a bowl with relish.

You could also add cooked chicken left over from the family meal to scrambled egg for elderly dogs and fussy eaters.

Minty Minced Lamb

A fragrant meal that will attract even the fussiest of dogs.

INGREDIENTS

3 mugs long grain rice

6 mugs water

2 cubes lamb stock

500g minced lamb

1 tsp garlic granules

4 tbsp dried mint

TO MAKE

➤ Place the rice into a deep pan and pour the water on top. Bring to the boil and then turn down the heat to simmer.

➤ Add the stock cubes, minced lamb, garlic granules and mint and continue to simmer until most of the liquid is absorbed and the rice is cooked.

➤ Allow to cool and serve.

Note: This recipe can be divided into dog-sized portions and kept refrigerated for several days.

Sardine Patties

Food as flavoursome as sardines will tempt even the fussiest of canine palates. Using store cupboard items, it is easy to make and filling. Use sardines in oil rather than sardines in brine or tomatoes.

INGREDIENTS

2 large potatoes

Knob of butter or margarine

1 tin sardines in oil

1 egg

2 tbsp vegetable oil

1 mug frozen peas and sweetcorn, defrosted

TO MAKE

➤ Peel and cube the potatoes. Place into a pan of salted, boiling water and simmer until tender.

➤ Drain the water, add butter or margarine and mash well.

➤ Drain the sardines, keeping the oil to one side. Mash the fish and add to the potato along with the defrosted peas and sweetcorn.

➤ Whisk the egg and add to the mashed potatoes. Stir well to combine all the ingredients.

➤ Turn the mixture out onto a floured board and divide into appropriately sized patties for your dog's mouth. Using floured hands, pat them into a flattish shape, 1.5 to 2.5 cm in thickness. Allow to stand for half an hour.

➤ Place the oil from the sardines into a non-stick pan along with the vegetable oil and heat. When the oil is sizzling, add the patties and cook on each side until golden brown.

➤ Allow to cool before serving.

Note: This dish is ideal for leftover potatoes and works with most types of canned fish. If you are using dried potato, add a little flour to make the mix firmer.

Willy Burgers

Pork mince is often overlooked when cooking for dogs. It is full of flavour and tastes different to the commonly used minced beef. Our William loved these and would eat them as a treat when he was in the last year of his life and was not so keen on his usual food. It's possible to pop a dog's medication into the cooled burgers without him realising. And they are also good enough to share with the children!

INGREDIENTS

1 mug pudding rice

250g (or one small tray) of minced pork

1 clove of garlic, chopped finely

1 carrot, peeled and diced finely

½ mug frozen peas, defrosted

1 small can baked beans

2 eggs

4 tbsp vegetable oil

TO MAKE

➤ Add the rice to a pan of salted boiling water and cook until tender. Drain and place in a large mixing bowl to cool.

➤ When the rice is cool, add the pork, garlic, carrot and peas. Mix well together.

➤ Drain the baked beans but retain the tomato sauce. Mash the beans and then add them to the burger mix.

➤ Beat the 2 eggs and add to the mixing bowl. Stir until all ingredients are blended together.

➤ Turn the burger mix out onto a floured surface and with well floured hands divide the mix into dog-sized burgers. The smaller the dog, the more burgers you will have. I prefer small burgers rather than large ones. Pat them into a thickness of about 1 ½ cm and round off the edges so that they do not break during cooking.

➤ Heat the oil in a non-stick frying pan. Add the burgers and cook on a medium heat until they are cooked through and brown on the outside.

➤ Place on kitchen paper to absorb any residue of oil and leave to cool.

➤ Serve with the tomato sauce from the baked beans dribbled on top.

Cheesey Pasta Fritters

Dogs love cheese, so these fritters will go down a treat.

INGREDIENTS

2 mugs pasta shapes

100g minced beef

100g cheddar cheese

2 tbsp plain flour

2 eggs

4 tbsp vegetable oil

TO MAKE

➤ Place the pasta shapes into a pan of boiling water and simmer until the pasta is just cooked through. Drain and allow to cool.

➤ Put the minced beef into a large mixing bowl and break up with a wooden spoon.

➤ Add the pasta and mix.

➤ Cut the cheese into ½ cm cubes and add to the mix along with the flour.

➤ Beat the eggs and mix them into the cheesey pasta to bind the ingredients together.

➤ Heat the oil in a non-stick frying pan.

➤ Add spoonfuls of the mix to the hot oil and keep turning each fritter to make sure that the cheese does not stick to the pan. When golden brown, remove the fritters and leave on kitchen paper to drain.

➤ Serve when cool.

Potato Fritters

Sweet potatoes make all the difference to this interesting recipe.

INGREDIENTS

3 eggs

½ mug low fat milk

4 tbsp wholemeal flour

4 large sweet potatoes

2 tbsp vegetable oil

TO MAKE

➤ Beat the eggs and then add the low fat milk.

- ➤ Mix in the flour.
- ➤ Wash and finely grate the sweet potatoes. There is no need to peel them first.
- ➤ Add the sweet potato into the egg and flour mixture.
- ➤ Heat the vegetable oil in a non-stick frying pan.
- ➤ Add spoonfuls of the fritter mix into the hot fat and cook, turning once to ensure that both sides of the fritter are golden brown.

Note: Try not to have the oil too hot during cooking or the fritters will burn while the insides are still raw.

Vegetable Fritters

This is a way to use up vegetables from your store cupboard, or cook a few more while making the family's meal.

INGREDIENTS

½ mug frozen peas	1 large potato
½ mug carrot, grated	4 eggs
½ mug frozen runner beans	4 tbsp wholemeal flour
1 small stem of broccoli	4 tbsp vegetable oil

TO MAKE

- ➤ Place the peas and grated carrot into a large mixing bowl.
- ➤ Chop the runner beans and broccoli before adding to the mixing bowl.
- ➤ Wash and grate the potato and add to the other ingredients.
- ➤ Beat the eggs and add to the vegetables along with the flour.
- ➤ Heat the oil and fry spoonfuls of the mixture, turning the fritters once to ensure they are golden brown on both sides.

Doggy Burgers

A burger with a crunch, which dogs will enjoy.

INGREDIENTS

250g minced beef
1 mug oatmeal
2 cubes beef stock

2 eggs
2 tbsp vegetable oil

TO MAKE

➤ Place the minced beef into a large mixing bowl and break up with a wooden spoon.
➤ Add the oatmeal and crumble in the beef stock cubes.
➤ Beat the eggs and add to the mixture. Use your hands to combine the ingredients.
➤ Take portions of the mixture and with wet hands mould them into burgers suitable for the size of your dog.
➤ Put the vegetable oil into a non-stick frying pan and bring up to heat.
➤ Fry the burgers on both sides until they are cooked through and place them onto kitchen paper to remove excess oil.
➤ Serve to your dog when cool, either dry or with gravy and mixer biscuit.

Salmon Hash

A tasty meal for your dog made from items found in most store cupboards and freezers.

INGREDIENTS

2 large potatoes
1 tin salmon
1 mug oats

2 large carrots
1 small tub natural yoghurt

TO MAKE

➤ Preheat the oven to 200°C/Gas Mark 6.
➤ Peel and cube the potatoes. Place into boiling water and simmer until soft. Drain and mash.

➤ Remove the salmon from the tin, retaining any liquid. Flake the salmon and add to the mashed potato along with the oats.

➤ Wash and finely grate the carrots. Stir into the potato mixture.

➤ Add the yoghurt and the liquid from the salmon tin and stir until all ingredients are combined, taking care not to break up the salmon flakes.

➤ Place in an ovenproof dish and cook in the oven for 45 min or until the top is brown.

➤ Allow to cool before serving.

Note: Any canned fish can be used for this recipe.

Quick Pasta Bake

This recipe is very easy to prepare while cooking pasta for the whole family.

INGREDIENTS

1 piece smoked haddock	1 small tub cream cheese
1 handful spaghetti	50g cheddar cheese, grated

TO MAKE

➤ Poach the haddock in a shallow pan of water for 5 min. Drain and retain the stock. Flake the haddock, taking care to remove any small bones.

➤ At the same time, place the pasta into a pan of boiling water and cook until soft, taking care not to over cook. Drain the pasta.

➤ Add the smoked haddock to the pasta along with the tub of cream cheese. Add some of the fish stock if the mix is too thick.

➤ Place into a heatproof dish and spread the grated cheese over the top.

➤ Place under the grill until the cheese is golden brown. Allow to cool, before serving to your dog.

Note: If you need to watch your dog's weight, use low fat cream cheese. Adjust the amount of pasta to the size of your dog.

Barbecue Chicken

My dogs just love barbecue sauce, so why make your own when it's there in the cupboard just shouting out to be used? I add stock as then there is also a gravy for the mixer biscuit.

INGREDIENTS

2 tbsp olive oil
1 standard-sized tray of chicken
   (approx. 250 g), diced

½ bottle barbecue sauce
1 mug water
1 cube chicken stock

TO MAKE

➤ Heat the olive oil in a frying pan and add the chicken. Turn often until the chicken is cooked through.
➤ Add the sauce, water and stock cube.
➤ Bring to the boil and simmer for 30 min or until the chicken is tender,
➤ Remove from the heat and allow to cool.
➤ Serve over homemade mixer biscuit.

Note: The Cheesey Mixer Biscuit is ideal for this recipe.

Rice and Egg Omelette

This is an easy and nutritious meal for a dog of any age.

INGREDIENTS

½ mug brown rice
1 cube chicken stock
1 clove of garlic
1 carrot

1 tbsp vegetable oil
½ mug runner beans
½ mug peas
4 eggs

TO MAKE

➤ Place the rice and stock cube in a pan, cover with boiling water and simmer until cooked. Strain and put the rice to one side.
➤ Chop the garlic.
➤ Wash and finely chop the carrot.

- ➤ Heat the oil in a deep-sided frying pan and add the garlic and carrot to the pan for several minutes, before adding the runner beans and peas. Stir fry until cooked through.
- ➤ Add the rice and heat through.
- ➤ Whisk the eggs and add to the pan.
- ➤ Cook for 4 min, then carefully turn and cook on the other side.
- ➤ Remove from the heat and allow to cool before serving to your favourite dog.

Doggy Bread Pudding

This is an excellent way to use up old bread. A portion of this dish can be served to your dog along with his meat meal, but watch the portion size or your dog will gain weight.

INGREDIENTS

Butter or margarine	¼ mug mixed peel
8 slices wholemeal bread	1 large cooking apple
4 eggs	Grated nutmeg
½ mug milk	Extra milk
½ mug brown sugar	

TO MAKE

- ➤ Preheat the oven to 190°C/Gas Mark 5.
- ➤ Grease a deep baking tin with butter or margarine.
- ➤ Butter the bread on one side and cut into strips.
- ➤ Whisk the eggs with ½ mug of milk.
- ➤ In a bowl layer the bread, butter side up, with the sugar, mixed peel and apple, finishing with a sprinkling of sugar and nutmeg. Tip in a little more milk if it looks dry.
- ➤ Bake in the middle of the oven for about 45 min until the top is golden brown.
- ➤ Allow to cool before feeding to your dog.

Note: This recipe is large enough to last several days or feed more than one dog.

Everyday Biscuits

INGREDIENTS

1 can chickpeas

2 mugs wholemeal flour

1 mug rolled oats

3 tsp garlic granules

½ mug bran

2 eggs

½ mug olive oil

4 tbsp runny honey

1 cube chicken stock

1 mug warm water

TO MAKE

➤ Preheat the oven to 180°C/Gas Mark 4.

➤ Mash the chickpeas and place in a large mixing bowl along with the flour, oats, garlic and bran. Mix well.

➤ Whisk the eggs and add to the mix, along with the olive oil and honey.

➤ Dissolve the stock cube in the warm water and stir into the mixture until you have a pliable dough.

➤ Turn out onto a floured surface and roll to a thickness of just over 1 cm. Using dog-shaped cutters, cut out as many biscuits as possible and place on a non-stick baking tray.

➤ Bake slowly for several hours until the biscuits are really hard.

➤ Allow to cool before serving.

Super Snacks

INGREDIENTS

¼ mug hot water

6 cubes chicken stock

1 sachet dry yeast

2 mugs tomato juice

3 mugs wholemeal flour

2 mugs wheat germ

TO MAKE

➤ Preheat the oven to 160°C/Gas Mark 3.

➤ Place the water and stock cubes into a large bowl and dissolve.

➤ Add the yeast and allow to stand for 5 min.

- ➤ Add the tomato juice, flour and wheat germ to form a stiff dough.
- ➤ Roll out the dough on a floured surface to ½ cm thickness. Cut into shapes and place onto a non-stick baking tray.
- ➤ Cook on the bottom shelf of the oven for 4 hours or until the biscuits are really hard.
- ➤ Cool before serving.

Cheese Biscuits with Vegetables

INGREDIENTS

1 large carrot	1 tsp garlic salt
½ mug frozen peas	1 mug wholemeal flour
200g margarine	Milk
½ mug grated cheddar cheese	

TO MAKE

- ➤ Preheat the oven to 190°C/Gas Mark 5.
- ➤ Peel and finely chop the carrot. Place in a pan of water with the peas and simmer until soft. Leave to cool.
- ➤ Cream the margarine and grated cheese together in a bowl.
- ➤ Add the vegetables, garlic and flour. Form a dough using a little milk.
- ➤ Cover in cling film and chill in the fridge.
- ➤ Turn onto a floured surface. Roll out to a thickness of 1½ cm and cut into shapes.
- ➤ Place onto a greased baking tray and bake for 20 min or until brown.
- ➤ Leave to cool.

Birthday and Celebration Food

Why should our dogs miss out on celebrating their birthdays? Any excuse is a good idea for cake and no doubt we all spoil our canine chums on their birthday. A chocolate fudge cake or a devil's food cake may be ideal for the owners but, sadly, for little Fido the ingredients are not such a good idea.

By making a cake that can be consumed over several days and from ingredients more agreeable to our little chums we are not filling them with nasty additives or shortening their lives.

Although these cakes and treats are designed to suit our canine chums' digestion, they should not be fed to excess. Try to feed sensibly and replace some of their daily meal with the treats. A few extra walks and a game in the garden should soon work off the excesses of the celebration – but not straight after a meal. After all, it's not every day a dog celebrates its birthday!

Be adventurous when decorating the cakes – make them bright and colourful. Finely grated vegetables, fruit slices, yoghurts, low fat cream cheese, carob and doggy chocs can all be used to great effect when finishing off that special cake. Personalise it by adding a little food colouring to cream cheese and pipe your dog's name and age. Paw marks, wagging tails and cartoon dogs copied from magazines can make delightful finishing touches to your canine work of art.

Never use currants or sultanas when making a cake for your dog. In addition, never decorate with grapes or chocolate made for human consumption. These ingredients can do untold harm to your dog's digestive system and, in fact, they can kill.

Healthy Beef Birthday Cake

Like most of the recipes in this book, this tasty cake can be adapted to suit the store cupboard and the availability of seasonal ingredients.

INGREDIENTS

1 mug brown rice
1 cube beef stock
½ small butternut squash
4 large carrots
1 head of broccoli
Small bunch of fresh parsley
1 mug wholemeal flour

1 mug oatmeal
1 standard sized tray of minced beef
  (approx. 250g)
1 small tray of ox liver
2 cloves of garlic
4 eggs
½ mug vegetable oil

TO MAKE

➤ Preheat the oven to 190°C/Gas Mark 5.

➤ Put the brown rice into a pan with the stock cube and cover with boiling water. Bring to the boil and simmer until the rice is cooked but not too soft.

➤ Meanwhile, wash the vegetables. Peel the butternut squash and chop all vegetables into evenly sized pieces and place into a food processor. Blitz until the vegetables resemble fine breadcrumbs and then add the parsley for a final 5 sec blitz.

➤ Place the finely chopped vegetables into a large mixing bowl along with the wholemeal flour and oatmeal. Mix together.

➤ Next, place the minced beef and the ox liver into the food processor and blitz along with the garlic cloves until you have a smooth paste. Add the eggs and mix well together for several seconds.

➤ Add this mix to the bowl and stir together well. At this point, stir in the cooked rice and add the vegetable oil until you have a mixture that is not too runny. It is not essential to use all of the oil. If the mixture becomes too wet, add a little more oatmeal to stiffen.

➤ Pour into a greased baking tin or two round cake tins and place in the centre of the oven. (The new style silicone bakeware is ideal for baking this recipe, as the cake will slide away from the container with ease.) Bake for 45 min or until a skewer comes out clean when slid into the centre of the cake.

➤ Turn out onto a cooling rack and leave to cool.

Victoria Sandwich Carrot Cake

INGREDIENTS

2 × 400g cans of a solid dog food such
   as Chappie
1 mug self-raising flour
½ mug porridge oats

4 eggs
1 mug grated carrot
¼ mug chopped parsley
½ mug vegetable oil

Filling
1 tub low fat cottage cheese

1 mug grated carrot

Topping
1 tub low fat natural yoghurt
½ mug finely grated carrot

½ mug finely chopped parsley

TO MAKE

➤ Preheat the oven to 180°C/Gas Mark 5.
➤ Wipe the inside of two sandwich tins with a little of the vegetable oil and dust with 1 tsp of the flour, shaking off the excess. (There is no need to do this if you use silicone bakeware.)
➤ Empty the canned dog food into a large mixing bowl and break into small lumps using a fork.
➤ Add the self-raising flour and porridge oats and mix well.
➤ Whisk the eggs and add to the mixture.
➤ Add the carrot and parsley.
➤ Add the vegetable oil a little at a time until you have the consistency of a cake mix. There is no need to use all the oil if it is not required.
➤ Divide evenly between the two cake tins and place in the middle of the oven.
➤ Check after 45 min. Pierce with a skewer and if it comes out clean then the cakes are cooked. If not, leave in the oven for another 10 min and check again. If you find that the cakes are browning on top but are very soft inside, reduce the oven's heat and cook for longer.

➤ When cooked, remove both cakes from the oven and turn out onto a cooling tray. While the cakes are cooling make the filling.

To fill
➤ Drain any excess liquid from the tub of low fat cottage cheese and then pour into a mixing bowl.
➤ Add the grated carrot and mix well. Cover and refrigerate until the cakes are cool.
➤ Sandwich the two cakes together with the cottage cheese mix.

To decorate
➤ Drain any excess liquid from the low fat natural yoghurt. Spread the yoghurt over the top of the cake.
➤ Decorate with the finely grated carrot and chopped parsley. Serve immediately.
➤ This cake may be refrigerated but use within three days. Do not freeze.

Hint: Use dog or bone-shaped biscuit cutters as templates when decorating the top of the cake with the carrot and parsley. Or write your dog's name and age by sprinkling the decorations.

Peanut Butter Pup Cakes

INGREDIENTS

3 mugs wholemeal flour
1 tbsp baking powder
2 cubes vegetable stock
1 egg

½ mug vegetable oil
1 small jar crunchy peanut butter
Water to mix
1 small jar smooth peanut butter

TO MAKE

➤ Preheat the oven to 200°C/Gas Mark 6.
➤ Lightly grease a muffin tin with vegetable oil
➤ Sift the flour and baking powder.
➤ Crumble in the stock cubes
➤ Beat the egg well and add to the mix.
➤ Stir in the vegetable oil and the small jar of smooth peanut butter. The mix should resemble a cake mix. If it is too runny add more flour. If it is too stiff add more water.
➤ Divide the mix into the muffin tin, taking care to only three quarter fill each section.
➤ Place in the middle of the oven and bake for 20 min or until a skewer comes out clean when slid into a muffin.
➤ Turn out onto a cooling tray.
➤ When completely cool swirl the top of each with the smooth peanut butter and serve to your pup.

Hungry Dog's Hummus

When organising a party for your canine chums, why not make tasty toppers for fancy dog biscuits that will tempt even the fussiest eater? Remember though that any extra treats given to your dog must be allowed for in his daily food consumption or you will soon need to be cooking from the calorie counting chapter!

INGREDIENTS

2 cans chick peas

3 cloves of garlic, chopped

½ mug parsley, chopped

4 tbsp olive oil

2 tbsp tahini

TO MAKE

➤ Place the ingredients into a food processor and pulse into a rough paste. Don't blend the hummus until it is too smooth or it will run off the biscuit.

➤ Serve on top of one of the tasty biscuits given in Chapter 2.

Cheesey Cabbage Pittas

INGREDIENTS

½ white cabbage

200g strong tasting cheese

2 cloves of garlic

1 large tub low fat natural yoghurt

Wholemeal mini pitta breads

TO MAKE

➤ Shred the white cabbage finely and place into a large bowl.

➤ Grate the cheese and mix with the cabbage.

➤ Chop the garlic and stir into the cabbage and cheese mix.

➤ Tip any excess water from the yoghurt and stir into the vegetable and cheese until you have a stiff consistency that is not too sloppy.

➤ Slit an opening in each pitta bread and lightly grill on each side until crispy.

➤ When cool, stuff each pitta with the cheesy cabbage mix and serve.

Canine Christmas Pudding

There is no reason why this tasty Christmas treat cannot be shared with our four-legged friends. However, we may find we need a little more sweetness than they do!

INGREDIENTS

6 plums
1 mug shredded vegetable suet
2 mugs brown breadcrumbs
¼ mug brown sugar

1 level tsp all spice
2 tbsp molasses
2 eggs, well beaten
½ mug milk

TO MAKE

➤ Wash the plums, remove the stones and chop finely.

➤ Into a bowl place the plums, suet, breadcrumbs, sugar and all spice. Stir well.

➤ Add the molasses and the beaten eggs, stirring well. Add enough of the milk to make a soft consistency.

➤ Cover and leave overnight in the fridge for the flavour to develop.

➤ Place the mixture into a large greased pudding bowl or two smaller ones. Cover with greaseproof paper and tie securely with string, making a handle with string on each bowl so they may be lifted without burning your fingers.

➤ Place into a steamer and steam for 1 ½ hours. Test with a skewer. If it comes out clean then the pudding is ready; if not allow another ½ hour.

➤ Turn out the pudding onto a plate before it has cooled too much or it will stick in the bowl.

➤ Serve the pudding cold and not heated, as the fruit and sugar content could burn your dog's mouth.

Apple Buns

These tasty munchy buns will tempt any hound. Vary the size of bun tin depending on the size of the dog you are baking for.

INGREDIENTS

4 mugs self-raising flour

1 tsp cinnamon

1 tsp nutmeg

4 tbsp runny honey

4 tbsp vegetable oil

2 eggs, well beaten

1 cooking apple

1 mug tepid water

1 mug oats

TO MAKE

➤ Preheat the oven to 200°C/Gas Mark 6.
➤ In a large mixing bowl combine the flour, cinnamon, nutmeg, honey, vegetable oil and eggs.
➤ Peel and core the apple and grate into the bun mix.
➤ Add enough water to make a thick cake mix consistency.
➤ Divide the mixture evenly into greased bun tins. Sprinkle the oats onto the top of each bun.
➤ Place in the centre of the oven and cook for 25 min or until a skewer placed into the centre of the bun comes away clean.

Note: For special occasions, use fancy cake cases for presentation but do not give them to your dog.

Celebration Muttfins

Yummy cakes for your dog's birthday tea party.

INGREDIENTS

1 mug plain flour	4 tbsp runny honey
1 mug porridge oats	1 egg
1 tsp cinnamon	3 bananas, mashed
½ tsp baking powder	1 tbsp vanilla flavouring
½ mug vegetable oil	5 tbsp milk

TO MAKE

➤ Preheat the oven to 200°C/Gas Mark 6.

➤ Add all the dry ingredients into a large mixing bowl and stir well.

➤ Gradually mix in the wet ingredients leaving the milk until last. Then stir in the milk until you have a thick dropping consistency.

➤ Place paper muffin cases into a bun tin and two-thirds fill each one with the muttfin mixture.

➤ Place in the centre of the preheated oven for 15–20 min or until a skewer comes out clean from the centre of a muttfin.

➤ Place onto a cooling tray and when cool store in an airtight container. They will keep for approximately 4 days, if they last that long!

Hot Dog Muffins

A really unusual muffin treat for doggy party guests.

INGREDIENTS

6 beef sausages	1 egg
1 mug wholemeal four	½ mug milk
1 mug self-raising flour	2 tbsp vegetable oil
½ tsp mustard powder	

TO MAKE

➤ Preheat the oven to 200°C/Gas Mark 6.

➤ Cut the beef sausages into halves and place under the grill until cooked and brown. Place onto a cooling rack and allow to cool.

➤ Put all the dry ingredients into a bowl and mix well.

➤ Beat the egg and add to the dry mix, along with the milk and vegetable oil.

➤ Put the muffin cases into a bun tray for support and quarter-fill each case with the muffin mix. Add half a sausage to each muffin case. Add more muffin mix so that each case is ¾ full.

➤ Place into the centre of the preheated oven and cook for 20 min or until a skewer comes out clean from a cooked muffin,

➤ Place onto a cooling tray and serve to guests when cold, remembering to remove the paper muffin cases first.

Note: You could decorate these muffins by scattering frozen peas or chopped carrot onto the tops before baking.

Ahhh! Lamb Birthday Cake

A tasty meaty treat for your dog's birthday dinner.

INGREDIENTS

500g lamb mince

4 eggs

2 carrots

Handful of fresh parsley

1 mug self-raising flour

½ mug porridge oats

¼ mug vegetable oil

Topping

1 tub low fat cream cheese

1 packet doggy chocs

TO MAKE

➤ Preheat the oven to 200°C/Gas Mark 6.

➤ Place the lamb mince into a large mixing bowl. Beat the eggs and stir into the lamb until well combined.

➤ Grate the carrots and finely chop the parsley.

➤ Add the flour, oats, vegetable oil, carrots and parsley to the lamb mixture. Stir until all ingredients are combined.

➤ Tip the mix into a deep cake tin – a silicone tin is ideal for dog cakes as they come out easily and the container does not need to be greased before use.

➤ Place into the centre of the preheated oven and cook for 45 min or until a skewer comes out clean from the centre of the cake.

➤ When cooked, place the cake in its tin onto a cooling rack. When cold, turn upside down to remove the cake from the container.

To decorate

➤ Spread the low fat cream cheese over the top of the cake and using a fork make peaks like snow drifts across the cake. Add doggy choc drops to the top of each peak, before serving to your birthday dog.

Lovely Layer Cake

This is not quite the layer cake we humans are used to but your canine chums will love it!

INGREDIENTS

6 eggs, beaten
200g margarine, softened
3 mugs self-raising flour
¼ mug vegetable oil
1 large jar chicken baby food

6 large carrots, finely grated
6 rashers streaky bacon
1 carton low fat cream cheese
1 large carton natural yoghurt

TO MAKE

➤ Preheat the oven to 180°C/Gas Mark 4.

➤ Grease and flour two 8 inch sandwich tins or use two silicone Victoria sandwich tins.

➤ Place the eggs into a large mixing bowl and beat in the softened margarine.

➤ Add the flour and stir well before combining the vegetable oil into the mixture.

➤ Add the jar of baby food and half of the grated carrot.

➤ Divide the mixture between the two sandwich tins and bake in the oven for 60 min or until the cakes are cooked.

➤ Place on a wire cooling rack until completely cold, then turn out the cakes.

➤ Grill the bacon rashers until they are hard. Allow to cool and then chop finely.

➤ Put the first cake onto a serving plate. Spread the cream cheese over the cake along with the remaining grated carrot. Place the other cake on top.

- Drain any excess fluid from the yoghurt and stir well before spreading over the top and sides of the cake.
- Decorate with the bacon pieces and serve.

Cottage Cheese Cake

This is an interesting recipe that your dog will love. I always use a large silicone-type cake tin for this recipe as the cake slides out cleanly and there's hardly any washing up required. Made from store cupboard basics, it can be prepared within minutes.

INGREDIENTS

10 eggs

2 large tubs low fat cottage cheese

2 tins value price corned beef

1 can new potatoes

2 tsp garlic granules

TO MAKE

- Preheat the oven to 220°C/Gas Mark 7.
- Break the eggs into a large mixing bowl and whisk well.
- Add the cottage cheese and beat until you have a thick, even mixture.
- Remove the corned beef from the tins and cut into cubes of approximately 1.5 cm. Scatter over the base of the cake tin.
- Drain and wash the new potatoes before dicing them up and adding to the corned beef.
- Sprinkle with the garlic granules and tip the egg and cottage cheese mix on top.
- Place into the oven and cook for 40 min or until the cake is brown on top and a skewer comes out clean when slid into it.
- Turn out onto a cooling rack and serve once cold.

Fruity Bars

These bars are so easy to make and are ideal for doggy birthday parties. Left to set, hard little teeth will enjoy chewing them.

INGREDIENTS

4 mugs oats

1 mug wholemeal flour

2 tbsp molasses

3 tbsp runny honey

2 sweet apples

1 small carton glace cherries

1 small packet dried apricots

TO MAKE

➤ Preheat the oven to 200°C/Gas Mark 6.

➤ Combine the oats, flour, molasses and honey in a large mixing bowl.

➤ Peel and roughly chop the apples and chop the glace cherries and apricots. Add them to the mix.

➤ Line a baking tray with greaseproof paper and spread the mix evenly on the tray.

➤ Bake in the oven for 1 hour. Then turn off the oven and allow to cool.

➤ Use a sharp knife to cut into bars or squares before serving to your guests.

Note: It is sometimes easier to drop portions of the mix onto the baking tray and bake individual Fruity Lumps instead.

Training Treats

Food is always a good training aid. It should only be given as a reward when your dog has been good and achieved a goal in his training. Keep the training treats to very small pieces so that the food given during a training session does not equal his day's food ration.

Purchasing dog treats as a training aid can be costly – they can also be full of additives and colorants. By controlling what goes into your dog's mouth, you are doing your best to keep him healthy and happy.

The treats should be smelly, tasty and interesting to your dog. Remember to praise him every time food is given as a reward. A pat on the back and a fuss as well as food is also a good idea. Gradually replace the food with a pat and praise so that food does not become the ultimate goal for your dog when he is good.

Wear clothes with pockets when training or perhaps a belt or bum bag with a pouch for the training treats. Your clothes can become quite smelly with the tasty morsels, so put the food into a plastic bag before it goes into your pocket or bag. Extra bags to pick up after your dog enables you to set a good example to other dog owners when attending training sessions.

Liver Lumps

INGREDIENTS

450g raw pig liver
1 egg

1 mug flour
1 tsp garlic granules

TO MAKE

➤ Preheat the oven to 200°C/Gas Mark 6.
➤ Blend the liver until it resembles a paste.
➤ Add the other ingredients and mix well.
➤ With floured fingers, make small balls of the mix and place onto a greased baking tray so that they do not touch.
➤ Bake for 20 min for soft treats or longer for a hard chew. Dust with more of the garlic granules for added flavour.

Note: Very small liver lumps baked almost solid make delicious training aids. To make chew strips, roll long strips of the mix in your hands and place on the tray to bake.

Peanut Marbles

These easy-to-make treats can be used when training your dog as they just love the flavour of peanut butter and will do anything for a taste. Keep the marbles small so that your dog stays slim.

INGREDIENTS

3 mugs wholemeal flour
2 tbsp baking powder

1 small jar crunchy peanut butter
1 mug milk

TO MAKE

➤ Preheat the oven to 220°C/Gas Mark 7.
➤ Combine the flour and baking powder in a large mixing bowl.
➤ In another bowl, mix together the peanut butter and milk until they are combined.
➤ Add the liquid mix to the flour and stir well. This should give you a firm dough-type mix.
➤ Pull marble-sized pieces from the dough and roll between your palms to form small balls. Place onto a greased baking tray and push the centre of each ball with your finger so that they are slightly flattened.
➤ Bake in the centre of the oven until brown and firm and then turn out onto a cooling tray.
➤ When cold, store in an airtight container.

Lamb Balls

Make these training treats as small as possible so that your dog does not gain weight while he is being trained.

INGREDIENTS

250g of minced lamb
1 egg

½ mug whole wheat flour
1 tsp garlic granules

TO MAKE

➤ Preheat the oven to 200°C/Gas Mark 6.
➤ Place all the ingredients into a food processor and blitz until you

have a thick dough-type paste. Add a little more flour if the consistency is too soft.

➤ Using floured hands, take small amounts of the mix and roll into balls.

➤ Place onto a non-stick baking tray and cook in the bottom of the oven until the balls are really hard.

➤ Remove and leave to cool on absorbent kitchen paper. Store in the fridge until needed. These balls may be frozen.

Note: Drain off any excess fat during the baking process so that the balls do not fall apart.

Cheesey Nibbles

This is a great way to use up old pieces of cheese and bread. It takes just minutes to prepare.

INGREDIENTS

4 slices of bread, any type will do   Any leftover hard cheese
1 tsp garlic salt

TO MAKE

➤ Place the bread into a food processor and blitz into fine breadcrumbs. Place the breadcrumbs into a small bowl and stir in the garlic salt.

➤ Cut the cheese into approximately 1 cm pieces and evenly space on a microwaveable plate. Heat in the microwave until the cheese is soft but not runny. This will take only seconds but the exact time depends on your individual machine. Remove from the oven.

➤ Drop individual pieces of soft cheese into the breadcrumb mix and roll between your fingers until the cheese absorbs the breadcrumbs and becomes firm.

➤ Place on a cooling rack until cold. Store in the fridge until needed and use within three days.

Fresh and Crunchy Treats

If it's fresh, it must be healthy! These quick to prepare training treats will be ready in minutes. Store them in a small polythene bag and they are ready for your pocket to take to training classes and dog shows. They are also ideal for training a dog at home.

When cutting up ingredients as training treats, you must judge the ideal size for your dog. What is correct for a Chihuahua would be minute for a St Bernard!

CARROT STICKS

Scrub the carrots and remove the ends and any blemishes. Using a sharp knife, cut them into small sticks. Dry on a paper towel and place into a polythene bag. Use the same day.

CHOPPED MEAT

Cooking a Sunday roast? Chop up small morsels of the meat and leave to cool. Chicken, beef and lamb can be very interesting to a dog when held in front of his nose during a training session.

APPLE CHUNKS

Use a firm apple such as a Cox or Bramley. Wash the apple and quarter. Remove the core and cut into bite-sized chunks. Store immediately and keep cool until needed. Use chopped fruit the same day.

Apples do discolour once cut and we would squeeze lemon juice over the pieces if preparing them for ourselves. However, many dogs will not take kindly to lemon juice and may back away if presented with food covered in juice. Dogs are not bothered if the apple has turned slightly brown.

CUCUMBER BATONS

This is another vegetable that should be used within hours of cutting or it will go limp and be hard to handle and unappetising to the dog. Wash the cucumber and halve. Scoop out the fleshy centre and discard. Slice into batons or cubes. Place in the fridge until needed.

Crunchy Bacon Frazzles

Who can't resist fried bacon? Your dog won't either when presented with this as part of his training routine.

INGREDIENTS

500g streaky bacon
1 tbsp barbecue sauce

Garlic salt

TO MAKE

- ➤ Preheat the oven to 220°C/Gas Mark 7.
- ➤ Cut the bacon into 2.5 cm pieces, removing any small bones.
- ➤ Place into a bowl along with the barbecue sauce and stir to coat the bacon pieces.
- ➤ Spread the coated bacon onto a non-stick baking tray and place in the top of the oven. Cook until brown and crispy, draining off excess oil as it forms.
- ➤ Turn out onto absorbent kitchen paper to dry.
- ➤ Sprinkle with a little garlic salt and leave to cool thoroughly before storing in an airtight container.

Crunchy Kidney Cakes

This is an unusual recipe but it's a tasty treat, easy to prepare and dogs just love it!

INGREDIENTS

500g kidneys
1 cube beef stock
2 tbsp vegetable oil

2 eggs
2 mugs whole wheat flour

TO MAKE

➤ Preheat the oven to 220°C/Gas Mark 7.

➤ Place the kidneys into a saucepan with enough water to cover them. Bring to the boil and simmer until just cooked. Remove from the heat and drain the kidneys, retaining the stock.

➤ When cool, place into a food processor and blitz until smooth.

➤ Add the crumbled beef stock cube and ½ mug of kidney stock plus the vegetable oil. Process for a few seconds until well mixed.

➤ Beat the two eggs and add to the mixture.

➤ Gradually add the flour until a thick mix is formed. Add more flour if necessary.

➤ Drop small spoonfuls of the mix onto a non-stick baking tray. Bake in the top of the oven until firm and brown.

➤ When cool, these kidney cakes can be frozen until needed. Or they will keep for 3 days in the fridge.

Tasty Cheesey Breadsticks

You can make these breadsticks into a longer size for a bigger treat, but left small they make ideal crunchy treats for training.

INGREDIENTS

1 egg

¼ mug cold water

2 tbsp vegetable oil

2 mugs whole meal flour

½ mug parmesan cheese

TO MAKE

➤ Preheat the oven to 190°C/Gas Mark 5.

➤ Break the egg into a bowl and whisk.

➤ Add the water and vegetable oil and stir.

➤ Mix in the flour and combine until you have stiff dough.

➤ Turn out onto a floured surface and knead for several minutes.

➤ Break off small pieces of the dough and roll them on the floured surface until you have the desired thickness to suit your dog.

➤ Cut into 2½ cm lengths and roll each stick in the parmesan cheese. Roll once more on the floured surface to embed the cheese before placing on a non stick-baking tray.

➤ Cook in the centre of the oven until brown, turning the breadsticks during cooking so that they cook evenly.

➤ Turn out onto a cooling tray and allow them to cool completely before packing in polythene bags for the freezer.

Tuna Cake Bites

Tuna, lovely! Any dog will come to its owner if he is promised a piece of this tuna cake. Made in the microwave oven, it won't be long before you have a delicious treat to entice your dog.

INGREDIENTS

4 eggs	1 tsp garlic granules
1 can tuna in sunflower oil	Plain wholemeal flour

TO MAKE

➤ Whisk the eggs in a large mixing bowl.

➤ Add the tuna and garlic granules and mix well.

➤ Gradually add the flour until you have a thick batter mix.

➤ Tip into a large flan-type dish that is suitable for a microwave oven.

➤ Cook for approximately 6 min depending on your oven capacity,

➤ Carefully turn out onto a flat cutting board and while still hot cut into small bite-sized pieces.

➤ Allow to cool before dividing into small bags and freezing until needed. When required, these bites can be popped into the oven to be crisped up.

Sausage Nibbles

Every dog loves sausages and these small nibbles will be a big favourite with your puppy.

INGREDIENTS

1 packet pork chipolata sausages	2 tbsp chopped parsley
1 tbsp runny honey	1 tbsp Hoisin sauce

TO MAKE

➤ Slice the chipolata sausages into small pieces.

➤ In a small dish mix the other ingredients. Add the sliced sausage and coat well.

➤ Cover with cling film and place in the fridge overnight.

➤ Preheat the oven to 220°C/Gas Mark 7.

➤ Drain the sausage pieces and place on a non-stick baking tray in the top of a hot oven for 20 min, turning once. When the sausage nibbles are brown, place the baking tray onto a lower shelf until they turn hard and crunchy.

➤ Allow to cool before use.

Sausage Balls

Sausage meat is a cheap meat product and so easy to work with. Make a batch and place some in the freezer for later. The added anise seed is so enticing to dogs that they will do anything for you!

INGREDIENTS

1 standard sized packet pork sausage meat

1 egg

1 tbsp anise seed

1 tbsp plain flour

TO MAKE

➤ Preheat the oven to 220°C/Gas Mark 7.

➤ Put the pork sausage meat into a mixing bowl and break up with a fork.

➤ Whisk the egg and add the anise seed and flour.

➤ Add the egg mix to the sausage meat and combine the ingredients.

➤ With floured hands take small pieces of the mix and roll it between your palms. Place them onto a non-stick baking tray.

➤ Bake for 25 min in the oven or until the balls are firm and brown. You may have to drain off any excess oil during cooking.

➤ When cool these balls can be frozen or kept in the freezer for 3 days.

Garlicky Chicken Treats

Garlic and chicken – delicious. These treats will drive your dog mad for more.

INGREDIENTS

2 chicken fillets

Garlic granules or garlic powder

TO MAKE

➤ Pound the chicken breasts until they are about ½ cm thick.

➤ Liberally sprinkle with garlic on both sides and cut into squares (the size depends on the size of your dog).

➤ Place in the microwave, cover and cook on high power for 2 min. Carefully turn and cook for another 2 min or until cooked through. (The length of cooking time depends on your microwave's capacity.)

➤ Leave to cool before placing in sealed bags and freezing.

Sage and Onion Treats

This is such an easy treat to make. You could even use left-over stuffing from the Sunday chicken.

INGREDIENTS

1 packet sage and onion stuffing

2 tbsp olive oil flavoured with garlic

1 egg

TO MAKE

➤ Preheat the oven to 220°C/Gas Mark 7.

➤ Tip the dry sage and onion stuffing mix into a bowl.

➤ Add the olive oil and enough boiling water to make a thick stuffing mix. Allow to cool.

➤ When cool, beat the egg and add to the stuffing mix.

➤ With floured hands take pieces of the mix and roll into small balls. Place on a non-stick baking tray in the centre of the oven for 20 min or until cooked and firm.

➤ Allow to cool thoroughly before placing in an airtight container and freezing for future use.

Kibble and Mixer Biscuit

Kibble

Kibble, or complete food as it is better known in the UK, is one of the most commonly-fed foods for dogs. Served in biscuit form and bought straight off the supermarket or pet store shelves and simply poured into the bowl, it is the equivalent of fast food for dogs. Some of these complete foods are very good, with manufacturers including only good wholesome ingredients. However, there are many complete foods that we should avoid unless we want our dogs fed on animal by-products, additives and preservatives. So what is the answer? Make it yourself of course!

This chapter provides a variety of kibble recipes that can be made daily for your dog or produced in bulk and stored in airtight containers, ready to serve whenever your dog needs feeding. The ingredients can be organic and wholesome, additive free or simply made from supermarket-own brands if you are on an economy drive. Adapt them to suit your dog, your views on nutrition or your purse.

I suggest you make and use the kibble each week and store it in an airtight container. Although it can be stored for longer, by making a weekly batch you are assured that the food is fresh and will not be wasted.

Mixer Biscuit

A mixer biscuit should be used in conjunction with meat to make the ideal meal for your dog. Whether the meat is raw or cooked or even a vegetarian mix, it will need the crunchy mixer to bulk the meal and make it even tastier.

When baking your mixer biscuit try to get it as hard as possible but do not burn it. This can be done by a long bake on a low heat, ideal in Aga-type ovens, or on a higher heat in a more modern oven. Practise and experiment until you are happy with what suits you, your oven and your dog.

Mixer biscuit should be stored in an airtight container once cool. Owning a large breed I get through an awful lot, so I make a new batch every few days. However, depending on the size of your dog and his food intake, the mixer biscuit can be kept for two weeks.

Basic Beef Kibble

INGREDIENTS

2 mugs wholemeal flour	500g raw minced beef
1 mug oats	1 mug beef suet or beef dripping
1 mug dried milk powder	3 eggs
2 cubes beef stock	1 mug water

TO MAKE

➤ Preheat the oven to 180°C/Gas Mark 5. Grease a selection of baking trays.

➤ Mix together the dry ingredients in a large bowl.

➤ Stir in the minced beef and the suet.

➤ Whisk the eggs thoroughly and add to the dry mix.

➤ Add enough water to form a firm dough.

➤ Divide the dough amongst the greased baking trays, pushing it down firmly until it is approximately 1½ cm deep.

➤ Place the trays into the oven and cook for 20 min. Then remove each tray in turn and score the half-baked mix into small squares. Return to the oven to continue cooking.

➤ After another 20 min, check the kibble and rotate the baking trays in the oven so that they cook evenly. Turn down the heat to the oven's lowest temperature and cook until the kibble is hard to the touch and lightly browned but not burnt.

➤ Remove the baking trays from the oven and leave on a cooling tray until cold. Turn out the hardened kibble and break along the score lines. When completely cool, store in airtight containers.

Note: Smaller dogs have smaller mouths so make the kibble slightly less than 1½ cm in depth and also score into smaller squares. Double or treble the ingredients for larger dogs or when you are baking in batches.

Turkey and Vegetable Kibble

INGREDIENTS

2 mugs wholemeal flour

1 mug oats

1 mug dried milk powder

2 cubes vegetable stock

500g minced turkey

1 mug vegetable suet

3 eggs

6 large carrots

1 mug peas

TO MAKE

➤ Preheat the oven to 180°C/Gas Mark 5. Grease a selection of baking trays and tins.

➤ Mix together the dry ingredients in a large bowl.

➤ Stir in the minced turkey and suet.

➤ Whisk the eggs thoroughly and add to the dry mix.

➤ Put the carrots and peas through a juicer, retaining both the pulp and juice.

➤ Add the vegetable pulp to the mix.

➤ Gradually add the vegetable juice until the mix forms a firm dough. If more liquid is needed, add water until you have the desired consistency,

➤ Divide the dough amongst the greased baking trays, pushing it down firmly until it is approximately 1½ cm deep.

➤ Place the trays into the oven and cook for 20 min. Then remove each tray in turn and score the half-baked mix into small squares. Return to the oven to continue cooking.

➤ After another 20 min, check the kibble and rotate the baking trays in the oven so that they cook evenly. Turn down the heat to the oven's lowest temperature and cook until the kibble is hard to the touch and lightly browned but not burnt.

➤ Remove the baking trays from the oven and leave on a cooling tray until cold. Turn out the hardened kibble and break along the score lines. When completely cool, store in airtight containers.

Lamb and Rice Kibble

INGREDIENTS

2 mugs wholemeal flour

1 mug oats

1 mug dried milk powder

2 cubes lamb stock

500g minced lamb

1 mug beef or vegetable suet

1 mug brown rice, cooked

3 eggs

1 mug water

TO MAKE

➤ Preheat the oven to 180°C/Gas Mark 5. Grease a selection of baking trays and tins.

➤ Mix together the dry ingredients in a large bowl.

➤ Stir in the minced lamb, suet and the cooled brown rice.

➤ Whisk the eggs thoroughly and add to the mix.

➤ Stir until the mix resembles a firm dough. If more liquid is needed, add water until you have the desired consistency,

➤ Divide the dough amongst the greased baking trays, pushing it down firmly until it is approximately 1½ cm deep.

➤ Place the trays into the oven and cook for 20 min. Then remove each tray in turn and score the half-baked mix into small squares. Return to the oven to continue cooking.

➤ After another 20 min, check the kibble and rotate the baking trays in the oven so that they cook evenly. Turn down the heat to the oven's lowest temperature and cook until the kibble is hard to the touch and lightly browned but not burnt.

➤ Remove the baking trays from the oven and leave on a cooling tray until cold. Turn out the hardened kibble and break along the score lines. When completely cool, store in airtight containers.

Chicken and Sweetcorn Kibble

INGREDIENTS

2 mugs wholemeal flour

1 mug oats

1 mug dried milk powder

2 cubes chicken stock

500g minced chicken

3 eggs

1 can sweetcorn kernels

½ mug vegetable oil

1 mug water

TO MAKE

➤ Preheat the oven to 180°C/Gas Mark 5. Grease a selection of baking trays and tins.

➤ Mix together the dry ingredients in a large bowl.

➤ Stir in the minced chicken.

➤ Whisk the eggs thoroughly and add to the dry mix.

➤ Place the sweetcorn into a blender and blitz until the kernels are broken down. Add to the kibble mix along with the vegetable oil.

➤ Stir until the mix resembles a firm dough. If more liquid is needed, add water until you have the desired consistency.

➤ Divide the dough amongst the greased baking trays, pushing it down firmly until it is approximately 1 ½ cm deep.

➤ Place the trays into the oven and cook for 20 min. Then remove each tray in turn and score the half-baked mix into small squares. Return to the oven to continue cooking.

➤ After another 20 min, check the kibble and rotate the baking trays in the oven so that they cook evenly. Turn down the heat to the oven's lowest temperature and cook until the kibble is hard to the touch and lightly browned but not burnt.

➤ Remove the baking trays from the oven and leave on a cooling tray until cold. Turn out the hardened kibble and break along the score lines. When completely cool, store in airtight containers.

Turkey Sate Kibble

This is an interesting recipe and an easy one to prepare. Even the fussiest eater will lick his lips when he tastes this!

INGREDIENTS

1 mug long grain white rice	1 jar smooth peanut butter
250g turkey mince	¼ mug light soy sauce
3 mugs wholemeal flour	2 eggs

TO MAKE

➤ Preheat the oven to 200°C/Gas Mark 6.

➤ Place the rice into a pan of boiling water, lower the heat and simmer until cooked. Drain and leave to cool.

➤ Place the turkey mince and rice into a blender and blitz until smooth.

➤ Put this mix into a large mixing bowl along with the flour and combine the ingredients.

➤ Put the peanut butter and soy sauce into a saucepan and over a very low heat stir until you have a smooth paste.

➤ Add this to the mixing bowl along with 2 beaten eggs. You should have a firm dough but if more liquid is required add a little water.

➤ Turn out into a non-stick baking tray. Using your hands, push the dough down and spread it over the tray right up to the edges.

➤ Bake in the middle of the oven for 60 min or until cooked through and very hard.

➤ Turn out onto a wire cooling rack to cool. When cold, break the biscuit into small kibble pieces suitable for your dog and store in an airtight container. Use within 3 days.

Cheesey Mixer Biscuit

Sometimes when a dog is poorly and off his feed we need to tempt him to eat. Cheese always seems to be a favourite and by baking it into the mixer biscuit you may well convince your dog to eat his meal. Try giving small portions and often until he is eating normally again.

INGREDIENTS

2 mugs white rice

4 mugs strong white flour

2 mugs oats

½ mug dried milk powder

350g strong mature cheese

3 eggs

2 mugs water

TO MAKE

➤ Preheat the oven to 190°C/Gas Mark 5. Grease two baking trays.

➤ Cook the rice in boiling water until it is not quite soft and still has a 'bite' to it. Drain and leave to cool.

➤ Mix the dry ingredients in a large bowl.

➤ Grate the cheese and add to the mix.

➤ Stir in the cooked rice.

➤ Whisk the eggs and pour into the mix.

➤ Add water as needed to mix to a stiff dough. Divide the dough into 2 pieces. Press each piece firmly into the baking tray until it is thin and flat.

➤ Bake in the oven for 45 min or until very hard. Leave to cool and then break into small pieces. Store in an airtight container.

This mixer biscuit can be served with raw meat or one of our cooked food recipes. It can also be used as titbits to tempt a dog or when training.

Garlic Flavoured Mixer Biscuit

The garlic in this mixer biscuit recipe gives more flavour to the accompanying meat meal.

INGREDIENTS

6 mugs wholemeal flour
2 mugs porridge oats
3 cubes beef stock
1 mug hot water

4 eggs
3 tbsp garlic granules
Cold water

TO MAKE

➤ Preheat the oven to 200°C/Gas Mark 6.
➤ Put the wholemeal flour and porridge oats into a large mixing bowl.
➤ Crumble the stock cubes into the hot water and stir until dissolved. Leave to cool.
➤ Beat the eggs and add to the flour and oats along with the stock. Continue mixing until you have a firm dough, adding cold water if needed.
➤ Turn out onto a floured surface and roll to ½ cm.
➤ Place the rolled-out dough onto a greased tray and score into squares of approximately ½ cm.
➤ Bake in the oven until really hard.
➤ Remove and allow to cool completely before breaking up. Then tip the biscuit pieces into a plastic bag and hit with a rolling pin to break up into smaller mixer pieces. Store in an airtight container until needed.

Oaty Crunch Mixer Biscuit

This is a slightly different mixer biscuit that can be made from store cupboard basics.

INGREDIENTS

1 mug rice	2 tbsp sesame oil
4 mugs oats	2 cubes lamb stock
1 mug wholemeal flour	2 mugs warm water

TO MAKE

➤ Preheat the oven to 200°C/Gas Mark 6.

➤ Place the rice in a pan of boiling water and simmer until cooked. Drain and allow to cool.

➤ Place the oats into a large mixing bowl. Add the rice and the flour and stir to combine. Add the sesame oil and stir.

➤ Crumble the stock cubes into the warm water. Stir until dissolved and add to the mix. Stir well until the stock is absorbed throughout the mixture.

➤ Tip the mixture onto a non-stick baking tray and spread evenly.

➤ Place in the top of the oven and cook for 30 min or until the stock is absorbed and the biscuit resembles the top of a fruit crumble. Stir several times during baking. The mix should be hard and crunchy.

➤ Remove from the oven and allow to cool before storing in an airtight container.

Note: I use a turkey tray for this recipe as the sides are higher than a traditional baking tray and there will be less spillage.

Fundraising and Presents

Home-baked presents for your friends' dogs show that you have put a little thought into what they really like. Here are some ideas for making personal gifts for canine chums.

Presentation counts, so why not put the biscuits or cakes into reusable containers. Fancy boxes or recycled chocolate boxes will hold cup cakes and Kilner jars are ideal for presenting training treats. A cake for that birthday puppy would look sensational in its own cake tin or even a cake box meant for a wedding cake. Your work will look professional and will be talked about for months after the party.

We all like to do our bit for fundraising events and sometimes it is hard to think of what to supply for the school summer fete or a fun day at your dog club. A cake stand just for dogs is a talking point and will attract buyers. You could make pretty packets of dog biscuits and small treats that can be taken home, or perhaps sell slices from a large cake for dogs to consume on the spot. Tray bakes are also a lovely idea, with customers buying slices of fruity doggy cake or perhaps savoury slices.

What about 'Guess the weight of the dog cake?' with the winner winning the cake of course! Cakes personalised for each dog are also a good idea as you can ice the names onto the cakes as they are bought – but practise doing this at home first!

If you decide to run a canine cake stall as a fundraising event, take along plenty of bags for the food to be taken home and be prepared to clear up around the stall afterwards where eager dogs will have dropped crumbs. Display the food as you would at your own tea party. Place cup cakes on tiered stands and borrow cake stands for the larger cakes. Paper bowls may be the answer for the 'buy one and eat it now' service.

Baking to raise funds is a great way to show that you care.

Christmas Ginger Cookies
Hang these cookies on your Christmas tree, but hang them high or lose them!

INGREDIENTS

2 mugs wholemeal flour	2 eggs
½ mug dried milk powder	2 tbsp vegetable oil
½ mug porridge oats	1 mug water
3 tsp dried ginger	15 cm lengths of thin red ribbon

TO MAKE
➤ Preheat the oven to 200°C/Gas Mark 6.
➤ In a large mixing bowl place the wholemeal flour, milk powder, porridge oats and dried ginger. Mix well.
➤ Beat the eggs and add to the mix along with the vegetable oil.
➤ Gradually add water to form a firm dough.
➤ Turn out onto a floured board and roll out to a thickness of ½ cm.
➤ Using Christmas and dog-shaped cutters, carefully cut out as many ginger biscuits as possible. With a piece of wooden doweling or the handle end of a wooden spoon, pierce a hole in the top part of each biscuit.
➤ Place onto a non-stick baking tray and bake in the centre of the oven for 35 min. Turn off the oven so that the biscuits become crunchy but not burnt.

➤ When cool, thread the pieces of ribbon through the pre-made holes in the biscuits ready to hang them on a Christmas tree.

Yummy Liver Tray-baked Brownies

This tray bake will lure every dog to your table. Serve by the slice straight from the tray.

INGREDIENTS

1½ kg liver

6 cloves of garlic

1 mug wholemeal flour

3 mugs plain white flour

4 eggs

1 small tub parmesan cheese

Garlic granules

TO MAKE

➤ Preheat the oven to 200°C/Gas Mark 6.

➤ Place the liver and garlic in a blender and blitz to a finely grained liquid. Tip into a large mixing bowl.

➤ Add the flour and mix well.

➤ Beat the eggs and add to the mix, followed by the parmesan cheese.

➤ Tip the mix into a greaseproof paper lined baking tray. You may need 2 trays, depending on their size. Spread the mix evenly in each tray.

➤ Bake in the oven for 40 min. Then turn off the oven and leave the brownies for another hour, making sure they do not burn.

➤ Remove from the oven and when completely cold turn out from the baking trays and remove the greaseproof paper.

➤ Put the brownies onto a clean baking tray and carefully cut into squares. Dust with garlic granules and serve to your customers.

Tasty Carob Cake

This is a lovely cake for fundraising as it can be sold slice by slice. Why not serve it on doggy print napkins or to be taken home in wedding favour boxes? Be warned: it is rather rich, so serve small slices.

INGREDIENTS

1 mug wholemeal flour	3 tbsp runny honey
2 tsp baking powder	2 eggs
½ jar smooth peanut butter	½ mug carob drops or chips
¼ mug butter	Extra carob or cream cheese

TO MAKE

➤ Preheat the oven to 190°C/Gas Mark 5.
➤ Put the flour and baking powder into a large mixing bowl and stir well.
➤ Place the peanut butter, butter and honey into a pan and warm on a very low heat until the ingredients have melted. Stir well. Allow to cool before adding to the flour mix.
➤ Beat the eggs and add to the mix. Stir to combine all the ingredients and stir in the carob drops.
➤ Place into a greased and floured cake tin and bake in the centre of the oven for 40 min or until a skewer placed into the centre of the cake comes out cleanly.
➤ Allow to cool before decorating with melted carob or cream cheese.

Note: Never be tempted to use chocolate meant for human consumption as it is extremely dangerous for dogs.

Vegetarian Biscuits

Cut out these biscuits using bone-shaped cutters and give them as prizes at charity companion dog shows or sell them to raise funds for your favourite dog club.

INGREDIENTS

2 large carrots	½ mug vegetable oil
1 mug frozen peas, defrosted	3 tbsp Demerara sugar
1 mug sweetcorn	3 cubes vegetable stock
3 mugs wholemeal flour	1 mug hot water
1 mug dry milk powder	2 eggs

TO MAKE

➤ Preheat the oven to 200°C/Gas Mark 6.

➤ Wash and roughly chop the carrots. Put them into a blender along with the peas and sweetcorn. Blitz until smooth and pour into a large mixing bowl.

➤ Add the flour, dry milk powder, vegetable oil and sugar. Mix well.

➤ Dissolve the stock cubes in the water and allow to cool.

➤ Beat the eggs and add to the mixture.

➤ Gradually add the vegetable stock until you have a firm dough.

➤ Turn out onto a floured board and roll to a thickness of approximately 1½ cm. Using bone-shaped cutters cut out as many biscuits as possible from the dough.

➤ Place onto a non-stick baking tray and bake in the centre of the oven until they are golden brown.

➤ Allow to cool on a wire rack before storing in an airtight container.

Tuna Cookies

Fish and cookies! What more could a dog want?

INGREDIENTS

1 mug rolled oats

1 mug wholemeal flour

1 tsp garlic powder

1 can tuna in sunflower oil

2 eggs

Water

TO MAKE

➤ Preheat the oven to 200°C/Gas Mark 6.

➤ Put the rolled oats, wholemeal flour and garlic into a large mixing bowl and stir well.

➤ Add the tuna and the oil from the can.

➤ Whisk the two eggs and add to the mix.

➤ Combine the ingredients into a thick dough. Add water if necessary.

➤ Take large pieces of the dough and roll into balls. It helps to dampen your hands whilst doing this. Place each ball onto a non-stick baking sheet and then using the back of a dessertspoon press the ball gently so that it flattens slightly.

➤ Cook in the centre of the oven until the cookies are brown. Remove and cool on a wire rack.

➤ Store in an airtight container and leave in a cool place. Use within 3 days of baking.

Doggy Muffins

Display these muffins at a fundraising event and they will sell like hot cakes.

INGREDIENTS

1 cooking apple

2 mugs wholemeal flour

½ mug rolled oats

2 tsp baking powder

1 small tub natural yoghurt

3 tablespoons vegetable oil

3 tbsp runny honey

3 eggs, beaten

200g cheese

Water

Extra runny honey

Carob drops

TO MAKE

➤ Preheat the oven to 190°C/Gas Mark 5.

➤ Core, peel and grate the apple.

➤ Put the flour, oats and baking powder into a large mixing bowl.

➤ Mix the yoghurt, vegetable oil, honey and beaten eggs in a smaller bowl until combined. Add the wet mix to the flour.

➤ Grate the cheese and add to the mix along with the grated apple. Stir well. It should have a thick dropping consistency. Add water if necessary.

➤ Drop enough mixture into each compartment of a non-stick muffin tray to half fill them.

➤ Place in the oven for about 25 min or until cooked. Remove and leave to cool.

➤ Drizzle a little honey over each muffin and decorate with carob drops.

Chicken Biscuits

Chicken stock gives these biscuits a delicious taste that dogs will love.

INGREDIENTS

3 cubes chicken stock

1 mug warm water

1 sachet dried yeast

4 mugs wholemeal flour

1 mug dried milk powder

1 tsp salt

1 egg

A little milk

TO MAKE

➤ Preheat the oven to 190°C/Gas Mark 5.

➤ Crumble the stock cubes into the warm water and stir until dissolved.

➤ Add the dried yeast to the stock and stir. Leave in a warm place for 15 min.

➤ Put the flour, dried milk and salt into a mixing bowl and combine.

➤ Add the yeast and stock mix and stir until you have a firm dough. Add more warm water if required.

➤ Turn out onto a floured board and knead for 5 min.

➤ Roll out to a thickness of approximately 1½ cm and cut into 5 × 5 cm squares. Place onto a non-stick baking tray and bake in the middle of the oven for 50 min.

➤ Remove the biscuits from the oven. Whisk the egg and milk together and brush the top of each biscuit with this mixture. Then return them to the oven.

➤ Turn off the oven and leave the chicken biscuits on the bottom shelf overnight to harden.

➤ Divide the biscuits into gift boxes for the lucky recipients.

Bacon and Parmesan Biscuits

You can use bacon off-cuts for this recipe.

INGREDIENTS

6 streaky bacon rashers	1 cube vegetable stock
2 mugs wholemeal flour	½ mug warm water
¼ mug parmesan cheese, grated	1 egg

TO MAKE

- ➤ Preheat the oven to 190°C/Gas Mark 5.
- ➤ Fry the bacon in a non-stick pan until cooked but not brown or crispy. When cold, blitz the bacon in a blender.
- ➤ Put the flour, cheese and bacon into a mixing bowl.
- ➤ Crumble the stock cube into the water and stir until dissolved.
- ➤ Beat the egg and add to the mixing bowl along with enough of the stock to make a firm dough.
- ➤ Turn out onto a floured board and roll to a ½ cm in thickness. Using fancy biscuit cutters, cut into shapes.
- ➤ Bake on a non-stick baking tray for 40 min or until brown and crispy.
- ➤ Place the biscuits on a wire rack to cool and then pack them into gift bags.

Cream Cheese and Chive Buns

INGREDIENTS

4 mugs self-raising wholemeal flour	2 eggs
1 carton low fat cream cheese	1 mug skimmed milk
1 tbsp dried chives	

TO MAKE

- ➤ Preheat the oven to 190°C/Gas Mark 5.
- ➤ Put the flour, cream cheese and chives into a mixing bowl and stir well to combine all the ingredients.
- ➤ Beat the eggs and add to the mix along with half of the milk. Add more milk if necessary to form a dropping consistency.
- ➤ Divide between the compartments of a greased bun tin, half filling each one.
- ➤ Place into the centre of the oven for 30 min or until a skewer comes out clean having been inserted into the middle of a bun.
- ➤ Place the buns onto a wire rack to cool.

Rice Carob Crispies

Cornflakes make an excellent substitute for Rice Krispies. Dogs love the crunch!

INGREDIENTS

4 tbsp golden syrup	1 mug carob pieces
1 tbsp butter	3 mugs Rice Krispies

TO MAKE

- ➤ Gently heat the golden syrup and butter in a pan until they have softened and combined.
- ➤ Remove from the heat. Add the carob and stir until melted.
- ➤ Gradually fold the Rice Krispies into the carob mix until they are well coated.
- ➤ Spoon portions into paper cake cases and allow to set before packing into presentation boxes.

Pumpkin Bites

This is an ideal recipe for Halloween celebrations.

INGREDIENTS

1 mug chopped pumpkin	½ tsp nutmeg
1 mug wholemeal flour	3 tbsp olive oil
1 tbsp brown sugar	2 eggs
½ tsp cinnamon	½ mug milk

TO MAKE

➤ Preheat the oven to 200°C/Gas Mark 6.

➤ Pulp the pumpkin and put into a mixing bowl along with the flour, sugar, cinnamon, nutmeg and olive oil. Stir well.

➤ Whisk the egg with half the milk and add to the mix. Add more milk if necessary to form a dropping consistency.

➤ Drop spoonfuls of the mix onto a greased baking tray and bake in the middle of the oven for 15 min or until cooked.

➤ Leave on a wire rack to cool.

Hot Dog Coolers

Dogs love to lick ice when the weather is hot. Always supervise these ice-licking sessions and make sure that your dog does not consume too many at once. In very hot weather the consumption of too much cold water can contribute to gastric torsion (bloat), so use these recipes with care. Use your own discretion when giving these cold treats to your dog; like any treat they should be served in moderation.

Icy treats can be used in the same way as training treats. By adding flavour to them there is added interest for your dog and a good reason for him to carry out the given command.

Collect small plastic containers left over from yoghurt, coleslaw and individual ice creams as they are just the right size for your hot dog coolers. Plastic disposable cups also make reusable holders for popsicles, while polystyrene cups can be peeled away from the yummy treats after they have been frozen.

Be careful where your dog eats his icy treats as they tend to slide all over the place and can make a mess. Outside in the yard or on the lawn is ideal as it keeps your floors clean.

Chicken Popsicles

This is an easy summer treat to make for your dog – ideally after roasting a chicken for the family's dinner.

INGREDIENTS

Leftover roast chicken pieces   1 mug hot water

1 cube chicken stock

TO MAKE

➤ Scrape the remaining chicken and skin from the carcass, making sure that you avoid any bones.

➤ Dice finely and divide amongst the sections of an ice cube tray.

➤ Crumble the stock cube into the hot water and stir until fully dissolved. Top up each section of the ice cube tray and place into the freezer.

➤ When frozen, remove the cubes from the tray and store them in a plastic container in the freezer. This frees up the tray for further batches of tasty popsicles.

Banana Bonkers

Dogs love banana and these treats freeze beautifully. Add them to flavoured jelly and they go down a treat.

INGREDIENTS

1 sugar-free lemon jelly   4 ripe bananas

TO MAKE

➤ Make up the lemon jelly following the packet instructions and allow to cool.

➤ Peel the bananas and slice lengthways. Line the banana halves up in a plastic container making sure that they do not overlap.

➤ Cover with the lemon jelly and place in the freezer until frozen.

➤ Remove the frozen block from the container and slice so that each piece has half of a banana.

➤ Place in a storage container and keep in the freezer. Use within 2 weeks.

Frozen Honey Yoghurt

Buying the large economy-sized cartons of low fat yoghurt will mean that you can make umpteen frozen yoghurt treats and always have one ready for your hot dog.

INGREDIENTS

1 large tub low fat natural yoghurt   Honey

TO MAKE

➤ Tip the yoghurt into a mixing bowl and place in the freezer until the yoghurt is semi-frozen.

➤ Remove and add small amounts of the honey. Mix it evenly through the yoghurt – the almost frozen yoghurt should keep the honey in small balls.

➤ Spoon the mix into tubs and freeze until completely solid. These portions can be turned out for your dog to chase around the floor until consumed or left in the plastic tub to be gradually licked clean.

Note: Take the plastic carton away from your dog as soon as it is empty as some dogs will chew them until they splinter.

Peanut Butter Suckers

Using ice cube trays for this treat will prevent your dog from consuming too much fattening peanut butter.

INGREDIENTS

Smooth peanut butter   Cold water

TO MAKE

➤ Fill an ice cube tray ⅓ with water and freeze.

➤ Remove from the freezer and spoon a little peanut butter into each section.

➤ Top up with cold water and return to the freezer.

➤ When completely cold, remove the cubes and pack into a plastic container or bag until needed.

Note: This recipe works just as well with molasses, golden syrup or honey, but use sparingly or you'll end up with a tubby dog.

Vegetable Popsicles

Vegetables and water – nothing fattening here, so these popsicles are ideal for dogs who are watching their waistlines.

INGREDIENTS

1 thin carrot	1 handful frozen peas
1 handful frozen beans	1 cube vegetable stock
1 handful frozen sweetcorn	Water

TO MAKE

➤ Wash and thinly slice the carrot.
➤ Place all the vegetables into a saucepan along with the crumbled stock cube and cover with water.
➤ Bring to the boil and simmer until the vegetables are cooked but still crisp. Remove from the heat and allow to cool.
➤ Divide the vegetables and stock between small plastic containers and top up with more water if necessary.
➤ Freeze until needed.

Fishy Ice Cream

This recipe may sound rather strange but your dog will love it.

INGREDIENTS

1 smoked haddock fillet   1 carton low fat readymade custard

TO MAKE

➤ Place the smoked haddock into a pan and add enough water to cover the fish. Bring to the boil and simmer for 10 min.

➤ Remove from the heat and allow to cool.

➤ Retain the fish stock. Remove the fish and flake finely.

➤ Meanwhile, tip the custard into a container and place into the freezer. When partly frozen, remove and beat well.

➤ Return to the freezer and repeat the process twice more, adding 1 tbsp of the fish stock each time.

➤ After the final beating, fold the fish into the custard mix and freeze solid.

➤ To serve, use a spoon or scoop dipped in hot water and slide it across the ice cream. This will create curls of the dessert rather than hard lumps.

Strawberries and Cream

My dogs love strawberries but if your dog is not so keen replace them with banana or pieces of apple. This is a dessert you could share with your dog. Add sticks and make tasty ice lollies!

INGREDIENTS

1 large tub low fat natural yoghurt   1 carton fresh strawberries
2 cartons low fat custard

TO MAKE

➤ Tip the yoghurt and low fat custard into a bowl and mix together.

➤ Clean the strawberries and chop into small pieces.

➤ Fold the fruit into the mix and make sure it is evenly distributed.

➤ Divide into plastic cups and freeze.
➤ When needed, dip the container into hot water and the treat will slip out easily.

Note: Flavoured yoghurt also works well with this recipe but try to purchase the low fat variety.

Frostee Paws

A blender is your friend here – a quick blitz and it's ready to freeze.

INGREDIENTS

2 bananas	4 tbsp honey
2 tubs vanilla yoghurt	2 tbsp smooth peanut butter

TO MAKE

➤ Peel the bananas and blitz them in the blender.
➤ Add the rest of the ingredients and mix with a few short pulses.
➤ Divide the mix between muffin cases placed inside a muffin tray. Freeze until solid.
➤ Turn out from the muffin tray and store in a plastic bag or container until needed. Remove the paper muffin cases before serving to your dog.

Choccy Drop Lickers

Never be tempted to use chocolate meant for human consumption – it could kill your dog. Carob drops or packets of dog chocolate drops should be used for this recipe.

INGREDIENTS

1 large tub low fat vanilla yoghurt   1 packet doggy choc drops
1 carton readymade low fat custard

TO MAKE

- Tip the vanilla yoghurt and low fat custard into a mixing bowl and stir well.
- Add the choc drops and stir again to combine the ingredients.
- Divide amongst ice cube trays. Freeze until solid.
- Turn out into a container and store in the freezer until needed.

Note: I find that pliable silicon ice trays make excellent containers for these treats as the choccy drop lickers slide out easily.

Toffee Sesame Ice

Sesame seeds and toffee – what dog won't like this treat?

INGREDIENTS

3 tubs toffee-flavoured low fat yoghurt   ¼ mug sesame seeds, toasted
2 sweet apples

TO MAKE

- Tip the yoghurt into a mixing bowl.
- Peel and core the apples and chop into small chunks
- Stir the apple into the yoghurt along with half of the sesame seeds.
- Tip the mix into a shallow tray.
- Freeze until the ices have set solid.
- To serve, turn out from the container and break into pieces. Scatter with the remaining sesame seeds and give to your dog.

Peanut Butter Ice Cream

INGREDIENTS
1 large tub natural yoghurt   3 tbsp honey
1 small jar crunchy peanut butter

TO MAKE
➤ Place all the ingredients into a large mixing bowl and beat until combined.
➤ Pour the mix into non-stick or silicon cake trays.
➤ Place into the freezer overnight or until frozen.
➤ Turn out each individual ice cream and store in a plastic container in the freezer until required.
➤ To serve, remove the required number of portions and place into a dog food bowl for 30 min to soften before giving to your dog.

Note: Humans love these as well!

Creamy Rice Licker
Just empty a few cans into a bowl, stir and your dog enjoys a tasty treat.

INGREDIENTS
2 cartons readymade custard   2 tubs low fat toffee yoghurt
1 can rice pudding

TO MAKE
➤ Tip the custard into a mixing bowl along with the rice pudding. Mix well.
➤ Carefully spoon a little of the mix into small cartons or bun tins.
➤ Add a spoonful of the toffee yoghurt to each dessert.
➤ Top up with the rice mixture.
➤ Freeze until the ices are solid.
➤ Turn out and store in a container in the freezer until needed.

Weight Control and Other Diets

It's so easy to over feed a dog. We need to be aware of everything that goes into their mouths and whether it is good or bad for them. Extra padding on the shoulders or not being able to feel their ribs or spine is a good indication that your dog is overweight. Lethargy and the inability to walk and run with ease means you have a problem.

Simply feeding a dog good nutritious food with no added fat goes some way to alleviating the problem. A brisk walk that doesn't distress your pet will help, but if he has been a couch potato in the past introduce added exercise gradually.

When feeding your dog treats, make sure they are part of his daily food intake and not an added extra and try to avoid giving titbits of biscuit and cake from your own plate.

We had a lovely little Polish Lowland Sheepdog called Oscar. He was half the size of our Old English Sheepdogs but could match what they ate each day with ease. Oscar's trick was to polish off his own meal, dash between the big dogs' legs and take a mouthful or two from each of their bowls before we caught him. He turned into a little solid tank of a dog and from then on we had to watch when we fed him and control his food intake – something we'd never experienced in the past. From then on, Oscar had his meals in his crate and stayed there for 15 minutes until the larger dogs had finished eating and their bowls were empty. Previously he had often picked up their metal bowls in his sparkling white teeth and run away with them, astounding the placid sheepdogs who always let him get away with it!

To aid his weight loss, we exchanged 75% of his mixer biscuit with fresh raw vegetables that had been put through a juicer adding both the vegetable pulp and juice to his meat. We found that if we just chopped the vegetables they came out his rear end mostly undigested so pulping worked for him. Before too long, Oscar was again the beautiful little dog we knew and loved and back to his slim, svelte, handsome self.

Sometimes the very opposite of a tubby dog can happen – some dogs have trouble putting on weight. As long as medical problems have been ruled out, it is down to you to find the type of food to body up your dog. Our Hayley was always too busy to eat her dinner – she always wanted to know what was happening around her and scoot off to play and have fun. She just about held her weight, but as a junior and in the show ring it was a problem. We had been given many tips, some of which were not good for dogs. I remember well the recommendation to give her mini Mars bars throughout the day – not only the wrong type of food for a dog but dangerous as chocolate can be a killer for dogs. We introduced meals on a little and often basis. Recipes such as the Skinny Dog Meaty Treats were introduced and she thrived.

At some time in his life your dog may be off his food due to poor health or while experiencing a season or even bereavement. Simply adding a tasty gravy or sauce to his meal will entice him to eat. Also try not to leave food lying around until your dog eats, as it can attract flies and in hot weather could start to turn. Little, often and tasty is the rule of the day. I have included some tasty sauces and gravies in Chapter 11. To encourage your dog to enjoy his meal, try making these recipes in batches and freeze single portions so that they are ready to defrost within minutes.

I cannot emphasise enough that any change in your dog's appetite or appearance should be checked out by a qualified veterinarian. However, I am also a great believer in speaking to your dog's breeder, who hopefully had years of experience before they even contemplated breeding a litter – if they didn't, can I ask why you bothered buying a puppy from them? Never buy foodstuff from a veterinary surgery, as they are there to treat dogs not trade as a grocer. Selling dog food is a big business and very profitable and sadly in most cases this is why it is sold by veterinarians. Profit is the consideration in these cases, not a dog's health.

Make your own dog food just as you cook from basics for your family and you cannot go far wrong.

Vegetable and Mince Meat Goulash

This is an unusual but interesting recipe that is easy to prepare.

INGREDIENTS

1 mug brown rice
Selection of fresh vegetables e.g.
   broccoli, carrots, white cabbage,
   green beans, asparagus

500g minced beef / turkey / chicken
2 eggs, beaten

TO MAKE

➤ Place the rice into a pan of boiling water and cook until tender. Drain and allow to cool thoroughly.
➤ Place the vegetables into a food processor and pulse down to a very fine consistency.
➤ Tip into a mixing bowl. Add the rice, eggs and minced meat and mix well together.
➤ Serve immediately with homemade mixer biscuit.

Note: If the vegetables are not pulverised down to almost a pulp, they will pass through your dog without him gaining any nutritional benefit from the food.

Fish Goulash
Any tinned fish will work in this recipe.

INGREDIENTS
1 mug brown rice

Selection of fresh vegetables e.g.
broccoli, carrots, white cabbage,
green beans, asparagus

2 tins sardines in tomato sauce

2 eggs, beaten

TO MAKE
➤ Place the rice into a pan of boiling water and cook until tender. Drain and allow to cool thoroughly.
➤ Place the vegetables into a food processor and pulse down to a very fine consistency.
➤ Tip into a large mixing bowl. Add the rice, sardines and eggs and mix well together.
➤ Serve immediately with homemade mixer biscuit.

Note: If you are catering for a smaller dog, halve the amount of ingredients.

Liver Goulash

Liver is another tempting food that will entice your dog to eat.

INGREDIENTS

1 mug brown rice
200g liver
2 eggs, beaten

Selection of fresh vegetables e.g.
broccoli, carrots, white cabbage,
green beans, asparaguS

TO MAKE

➤ Place the rice into a pan of boiling water and cook until tender. Drain and allow to cool thoroughly.

➤ Poach the liver in a little water until just cooked through. Drain and leave to cool, keeping the stock from the liver.

➤ Place the vegetables and liver into a food processor and pulse down to a very fine consistency.

➤ Tip into a large mixing bowl. Add the rice and eggs and mix well together. Add a little of the liver stock.

➤ Serve immediately with homemade mixer biscuit.

Note: If you are catering for a small dog, halve the amount of ingredients.

Poorly Dog Dinner

There are times when our little friends are poorly and not keen to eat. This tasty meal of chicken and rice will tempt them and not upset fragile digestive systems. It can be spoon fed if required.

INGREDIENTS

2 chicken thighs (leave the skin on)
1 stalk celery, chopped thickly
1 carrot, peeled and sliced

1 potato, peeled and cubed
1 mug white rice

TO MAKE

➤ Place the chicken and vegetables into a large pan. Cover with water and bring to the boil. Lower the heat, cover and simmer

for 2 hours.
- ➤ Add the rice and cook for a further 20 min until the rice is tender and has absorbed the liquid.
- ➤ Remove the chicken bones and dice the meat and skin. Return to the pan and mix well.
- ➤ Serve once cool or freeze for future use.

Note: I have used this recipe when my dogs have been very poorly. I pulse the dish down to a soup consistency in a food processor and then use a wide syringe (without the needle) to feed small amounts to the dog.

Skinny Dog's Meaty Treats
This is an easy recipe to prepare that will fatten up a skinny dog.

INGREDIENTS
250g pack fatty minced beef   Small tin condensed milk
1 mug wheat flakes

TO MAKE
- ➤ Preheat the oven to 200°C/Gas Mark 6.
- ➤ Place the minced beef and wheat flakes into a bowl and mix together.
- ➤ Gradually add the condensed milk until you have a fairly stiff mix.
- ➤ After flouring your hands, take small amounts of the mix and roll it into balls. The size of the ball depends on the size of the dog eating them.
- ➤ Place the balls onto a greased baking tray and cook in the centre of the oven for around 30 min or until cooked through.

These tasty balls can be hand fed to fussy dogs as treats so that they are consuming more calories and body up quicker. If you are feeding to a dog of a good size, then use them as a meal replacement.

High Taste Low Fat Biscuits

Any food can increase a pet's weight if he is over fed. These green coloured biscuits are low in fat and make a tasty treat for any dog watching his waistline if they are fed as part of a diet.

INGREDIENTS

1 can chickpeas	2 cubes chicken stock
½ mug spinach	½ mug warm water
3 mugs wholemeal flour	

TO MAKE

➤ Preheat the oven to 190°C/Gas Mark 5.

➤ Drain the chickpeas and rinse with cold water. Place into a food processor with the spinach. Blend until you have a smooth paste.

➤ Add the wholemeal flour and mix together.

➤ Dissolve the stock cubes in the warm water and then add to the mix until you have a firm dough.

➤ Turn out onto a floured surface and roll to a thickness of 2½ cm. Using biscuit cutters, cut out as many biscuit shapes as possible.

➤ Place onto a non-stick tray and bake for 30 min or until crisp. Turn out onto a cooling tray.

➤ Store in an airtight container and use within 5 days.

Veggie Snaps

These are an ideal treat for the dog that needs to watch his waistline. All the same, don't be too generous when handing them over to your drooling dog.

INGREDIENTS

½ mug water

3 tbsp vegetable oil

2 mugs wholewheat flour

1 mug white flour

2 celery stalks

1 red pepper

2 carrots

1 clove of garlic

TO MAKE

➤ Preheat the oven to 180°C/Gas Mark 4.

➤ Pour the water and oil into a mixing bowl. Add the flour.

➤ Finely chop the celery, pepper, carrots and garlic and add to the mix. Mix together well.

➤ Turn out onto a floured surface and knead for 5 min.

➤ Roll out to a thickness of ½ cm.

➤ Using a biscuit cutter, cut out the shapes and place onto a non-stick baking tray. Pierce each biscuit several times with a fork.

➤ Bake in the middle of the oven for approximately 30 min or until brown and crispy.

➤ Once cool, these treats can be stored in an airtight container and fed when required.

Cheesey Chomps

Use a low fat spread that is suitable for baking when cooking for your dog. It's ideal for the family as well.

INGREDIENTS

1 mug low fat cheese, grated
4 mugs whole wheat flour
4 tbsp dried milk powder
1 tbsp low fat spread

1 can baked beans
1 cube vegetable stock
1 mug hot water

TO MAKE

➤ Preheat the oven to 180°C/Gas Mark 4.

➤ Place the cheese, flour and dried milk powder into a mixing bowl. Rub in the low fat spread.

➤ Drain the excess tomato sauce from the baked beans and mash them into a paste. Retain the tomato sauce. Add the mashed beans to the mixing bowl and mix well.

➤ Crumble the stock cube into the hot water and stir until fully dissolved.

➤ Add the tomato sauce from the baked beans followed by the stock until you have a firm dough mix.

➤ Turn out onto a floured surface and knead for several minutes. Roll out to a thickness of ½ cm.

➤ Prick all over with a fork before cutting into shapes to suit the size of your dog.

➤ Place onto a non-stick baking tray and cook in the middle of the oven until brown.

➤ When cool, store in an airtight container.

Layered Potato Bake

This low fat meal should be served with lots of finely chopped raw vegetables to keep your dog slim and healthy. Mixer biscuit can be used sparingly.

INGREDIENTS

3 large potatoes
1 medium tub cottage cheese
½ mug cabbage, chopped and cooked
2 carrots, grated

½ mug low fat milk
¼ mug low fat cheese, grated
½ tsp garlic granules

TO MAKE

➤ Preheat the oven to 190°C/Gas Mark 5.
➤ Slice the potatoes and boil until tender. Drain and allow to cool slightly.
➤ Blitz the cottage cheese in a food processor until smooth.
➤ In an ovenproof dish, layer the potatoes, cabbage, cottage cheese and carrots. Pour the milk over the mixture.
➤ Sprinkle the cheese and garlic granules on top and cook in the top of the oven for 20 min or until the cheese is brown and bubbling.
➤ Allow to cool before serving to your dog.

Pile the Weight On Snacks

These tasty meatballs will help add weight onto a skinny dog. Feed them as treats rather than as a meal.

INGREDIENTS

500g minced lamb   1 cube lamb stock
1 mug rolled oats   1 tub parmesan cheese
3 eggs

TO MAKE

➤ Preheat the oven to 200°C/Gas Mark 6.
➤ Place the minced lamb into a large mixing bowl and break up with a fork. Stir in the rolled oats.
➤ Beat the eggs and add to the meat mix along with the crumbled stock cube.
➤ Combine the ingredients and using your fingers pull off pieces from the mix and roll into balls.
➤ Tip the parmesan cheese onto a saucer and roll each meat ball in the cheese so that it is well coated.
➤ Place onto a non-stick baking tray and cook in the centre of the oven for 30 min or until the snacks are brown and cooked through.
➤ Turn out onto a rack to cool and then open freeze by placing the snacks onto a tray, making sure they do not touch one another, and then freezing. Once frozen they can be stored in bags or containers.
➤ Remove the snacks from the freezer when needed and defrost before feeding to your dog.

Natural Breakfast

We have all come across the raw and natural diets that are advocated for our dogs' wellbeing. This recipe is for owners who would like to try a natural meal for their pet. The Natural Dinner recipe follows.

INGREDIENTS

2 mugs rolled oats	1 celery stick
½ mug natural yoghurt	1 sweet apple
1 carrot	1 tsp flax seed oil
1 broccoli stem	1 tsp kelp powder

TO MAKE

➤ Place the oats in a bowl and cover with the yoghurt. Cover and soak overnight.

➤ Juice the carrot, broccoli, celery and apple. Add the pulp and juice to the soaked oats.

➤ Stir in the flax seed oil and kelp and serve.

Note: This serves a medium to large dog, so halve the ingredients for a smaller dog.

Natural Dinner

This healthy meal may seem very fiddly to prepare but once you have all the ingredients it takes no time at all to prepare. Adjust the quantities to suit the size of your dog.

INGREDIENTS

250g raw beef	1 tsp flax oil
1 raw egg, beaten	1 tbsp cider vinegar
1 small tub cottage cheese	1 tsp kelp powder
1 tsp honey	1 vitamin C tablet, crushed

TO MAKE

➤ Chop the meat to a size suitable for your dog.

➤ Place all the ingredients into your dog's bowl and mix together.

➤ Add some homemade kibble or mixer biscuit and serve. Pulped fresh vegetables can also be added.

Note: Other kinds of raw meat can be added instead of beef, but avoid using liver more than twice a week as it can make some dogs loose.

Sauces and Gravies

Sometimes our dogs are so fussy we just don't know how to get them to eat. Pouring gravy over the food does work, but why not make sauces for your dog instead? Sauces are also a great way to fatten up a skinny dog.

As well as trying the recipes on the following pages, try saving some meat and vegetables from the family's main meal and blitzing them in a blender. Fork the sauce through your dog's dinner and he will eat every little bit.

Sauces for dogs' meals do not take long to prepare and can be served fresh, or frozen in small batches ready for days when the family has a takeaway or eats out and you are not cooking at home.

Chicken Liver Gravy

Chicken livers can be found in small tubs in the freezer section of most major supermarkets. I've used butter in this recipe to add flavour that will entice your dog to eat.

INGREDIENTS

1 tbsp butter
½ small onion, finely chopped
2 cloves of garlic
2 tubs chicken livers

2 cubes chicken stock
4 mugs water
2 tsp corn flour

TO MAKE

- Melt the butter in a heavy-based frying pan. Add the onion to the pan and fry until soft.
- Add the garlic and stir for 2 min.
- Add the chicken livers and fry slowly until just coloured. Remove from the heat to cool.
- Place the contents of the pan into a blender and blitz until smooth.
- Return to the pan adding the stock cubes and water, and simmer.
- Place the corn flour in a small bowl and add a little water. Mix to a paste and then add to the liver mix. Stir until the liquid thickens.
- Remove the gravy from the heat and allow to cool before placing into portion-sized containers and freezing.
- To use, remove from the freezer and warm through. Pour over your dog's dinner.

Sardine Surprise

This recipe makes a quick and easy sauce from store cupboard basics. Any dog will eat when he has the interesting aroma of fish to entice him.

INGREDIENTS

1 can sardines in tomato sauce   1 mug water
2 tsp corn flour

TO MAKE

- Place the sardines and tomato sauce into a saucepan and mash the fish with a fork. Add the water.
- Mix the corn flour with 2 tbsp of water until smooth. Add to the fish mix.
- Stir the sauce over a low heat until it warms through and thickens.
- Allow to cool before mixing in with your dog's dinner.

Stewed Lamb Gravy

The delicious aroma of lamb will have your dog dribbling and eager to eat.

INGREDIENTS

1 tbsp vegetable oil

1 clove of garlic, chopped

250g minced lamb

1 tsp rosemary, chopped

1 cube lamb stock

3 mugs water

1 tbsp gravy granules

TO MAKE

➤ Heat the oil in a heavy-based frying pan. Add the garlic and minced lamb. Stir until the lamb has browned.

➤ Add the rosemary, followed by the crumbled stock cube and water.

➤ Simmer for 15 min.

➤ Add the gravy granules to thicken.

➤ Allow to cool and then place in a blender and blitz until smooth.

➤ Divide into portion sizes and freeze until needed.

Curried Beef Sauce

A light curry sauce will have your dog eating in no time. Try using the minced beef found in the freezer section of your supermarket – it flows easily and is fine enough not to need blitzing in the blender.

INGREDIENTS

1 tbsp vegetable oil

250g minced beef

½ onion, finely chopped

1 tsp medium curry powder

1 tsp garlic granules

1 cube beef stock

2 mugs water

1 tbsp gravy granules

TO MAKE

➤ Heat the oil in a pan and add the minced beef, stirring so that there aren't any lumps.

- Add the onion along with the curry powder, garlic granules and crumbled stock cube.
- Cook for 3 min before adding the water. Simmer for 15 min.
- Add the gravy granules to thicken the mix. If the sauce is too lumpy, blitz it in the blender until smooth.
- Remove from the heat and allow to cool before freezing in dog meal-sized portions.

Egg 'n' Bacon with Brown Sauce

If your dog enjoys titbits from your breakfast plate, why not give him his own as a sauce. He is sure to eat his meal if it reminds him of his owner's meals.

INGREDIENTS

1 egg
4 rashers streaky bacon
1 tsp vegetable oil

1 small can baked beans
1 tbsp brown sauce

TO MAKE

- Boil the egg in its shell and place in cold water to cool.
- Remove any rind from the bacon and chop into small pieces before frying in the vegetable oil. Remove from the heat.
- Add the baked beans and brown sauce.
- Place into a blender and blitz until smooth.
- Remove the shell from the egg and roughly chop. Add to the bacon and bean mix and serve.

Chicken and Vegetable Sauce

This is an ideal sauce to make from chicken left over from a roast dinner. I often use a one portion-sized bag of mixed vegetables, which can be found in your supermarket's freezer section.

INGREDIENTS

½ mug white rice

1 mug cooked chicken meat, chopped

1 portion sized-bag of mixed frozen
    vegetables, defrosted (e.g. peas,
    runner beans, carrots)

2 mugs water

1 cube chicken stock

2 tbsp chicken gravy granules

TO MAKE

➤ Cook the rice in boiling water until soft. Drain and place into a mixing bowl.

➤ Add the chopped chicken meat and the defrosted vegetables. Stir to mix.

➤ Place the water and stock cube into a saucepan and bring to the boil. Add the rice, chicken and vegetable mix. Stir well and simmer for 5 min.

➤ Add the gravy granules to thicken.

➤ Remove from the heat and when cool blitz in the blender to make a thick, smooth sauce.

➤ Serve over your dog's meal.

Potato and Cauliflower Sauce

With this recipe, please remember that cheese can be fattening and should be used sparingly unless your dog needs fattening up.

INGREDIENTS

1 large potato, peeled and cubed

6 cauliflower florets

½ tsp nutmeg, grated

2 tbsp corn flour

1 mug milk

1 mug water

150g cheddar cheese

TO MAKE

- ➤ Place the potato and cauliflower florets into a pan of boiling water and simmer until tender. Drain and leave to one side.
- ➤ Place the nutmeg and corn flour into a small bowl and add 2 tbsp of water. Mix to a smooth paste.
- ➤ Place the milk and water in a pan and bring to the boil. Add the corn flour paste to thicken.
- ➤ Remove from the heat. Add the grated cheese and stir. Then add the potato and cauliflower.
- ➤ When cool, place into a blender and blitz until smooth.
- ➤ Use at once.

Sausage Sauce

Save a sausage when cooking for the family and this tasty sauce will entice even the fussiest eater.

INGREDIENTS

1 sausage, cooked   2 tbsp tomato paste
1 can chopped tomatoes   1 tsp garlic granules

TO MAKE

- ➤ Chop the sausage into bite-sized pieces
- ➤ Place the chopped tomatoes, tomato paste and garlic granules into a pan and warm through. The tomato paste will thicken the sauce.
- ➤ Add the chopped sausage and serve.

Note: Any kind of leftover cooked meat could be used for this recipe.

Ham and Pasta Sauce

This recipe can be made from leftover pasta and will help to fatten up a faddy eater.

INGREDIENTS

1 mug pasta shapes
1 can chopped tomato
1 tsp chopped herbs

2 tbsp tomato paste
2 slices boiled ham
1 tbsp parmesan cheese

TO MAKE

➤ Place the pasta shapes into a pan of boiling water and simmer until cooked. Drain the water from the pasta.
➤ Add the chopped tomato, dried herbs and tomato paste and simmer to thicken.
➤ Chop the ham and add to the sauce.
➤ Allow the sauce to cool and blitz until smooth.
➤ Stir in the parmesan cheese and serve over your dog's biscuits.

Sweet Sauce

Sometimes a dog prefers sweet food so, if he likes it, why not pour this sauce over his dinner? Dogs are not fussy about eating their main meal and their dessert at the same time!

INGREDIENTS

2 sweet apples
1 tbsp butter
Pinch of cinnamon

1 tbsp brown sugar
2 vanilla yoghurts

TO MAKE

➤ Peel and core the apples and chop finely.
➤ Melt the butter in a saucepan. Add the apple, cinnamon and brown sugar. Stir until the apple is soft.
➤ Put to one side to cool.
➤ Tip the vanilla yoghurt into a bowl and stir in the apple mix.
➤ Serve at once.

Foods that Are Dangerous for Dogs

When baking for our four-legged friends we must be very careful that we don't make them ill or, worse, feed them food that is poisonous. This chapter lists the most common foods that are dangerous for dogs, but if you are unsure about any type of food's affect leave it out of the recipe and make enquiries before it proves fatal.

Mention dogs and toxic food, and myths and urban legends start to circulate. 'Carrots are killers' is my favourite. Well yes, they would be if you were stabbed through the heart with one, but in normal circumstances a raw carrot is a low calorie treat for a tubby dog and helps to clean his teeth. Give one to a dog that has a tendency to swallow his food whole and it could possibly cause an obstruction – but then so could any food!

Alcohol

Some owners think it's a joke to give their dogs beer or let them finish off the dregs from glasses after a party. Firstly, dogs are much smaller than us and can get drunk much quicker on a lot less alcohol. They obviously cannot understand the effects of being drunk, so can become very frightened as their bodies are affected by the alcohol. They cannot walk or stand and are then very sick. What some owners do not realise is that alcohol is toxic to a dog, as after they feel similar sensations as those felt by humans a dog can fall into a coma and die.

Avocado

The high fatty content of avocado can cause stomach problems, vomiting and, in severe cases, pancreatitis. Persin, which is found in avocados, is toxic to a dog and can damage the heart and lungs. Furthermore, the large seed found in the centre of an avocado can be swallowed by your pet and become lodged in the throat or intestines.

Caffeine

Drinks containing caffeine may contain the chemicals theobromine or theophylline, which are toxic to a dog and can cause damage to the heart and nervous system.

Chocolate

As little as 57 g of chocolate with a high cocoa content can be fatal for a dog, due to the theobromide it contains. The higher the cocoa content, the higher its toxicity, so white chocolate is not as potent as a very dark quality chocolate. Sadly, having being fed chocolate, a dog will experience a great deal of pain, sickness and seizures before he dies.

Do not cook with chocolate for dogs – use carob or doggy choc drops. Even 170 g could be fatal to a dog of 20 k. Seek medical attention at once should your dog ingest chocolate.

Note that the bark chippings in your garden could possibly be cocoa bark, which is toxic to a dog. Ask at your garden centre before purchasing such a product.

Cooked Bones

Cooked bones should never be given to a dog. Cooking softens the bone and it may splinter, pierce internal organs and cause fatality. A raw meaty bone is much more beneficial to a dog.

Corn Cobs

It is so tempting to throw a corn cob to your dog after eating the fleshy sweet corn oneself. Beware: the cob can cause internal obstructions or choke the dog if he swallows large pieces.

Fruit Pips and Stones

Pips or stones from fruit such as apples, cherries, peaches, plums, pears and apricots contain cyanide, which is fatal to a dog. Fruit stones can also choke a dog or become lodged internally and cause great pain – possibly even death.

Garlic

There seems to be a great debate about the toxicity of garlic and its affect on dogs. Garlic is a natural cleanser and works well in our battle against fleas. It is the over use of garlic that can cause problems. By 'over use' we are talking about feeding more than one bulb to a dog – but we are never going to add that much to our dog's dinner are we?

I have used garlic capsules for many years with no ill effects on my dogs. They can be obtained from high street stores such as Holland and Barrett. It is not necessary to purchase the brands recommended for dogs as the prices are quite often highly inflated.

Grapes and Raisins

Grapes and raisins can cause serious damage to a dog's kidneys – fatal in fact. It is so easy to throw a few to a begging dog, but please stop and think before sharing such foods.

Macadamia Nuts

While not fatal, macadamia nuts can cause serious illness.

Onions

Onion can cause anaemia in dogs. Be careful when feeding readymade meals meant for babies or adults as they may include large amounts of onion. A very small quantity can be used for flavouring a dish.

Sweeteners

Sugar-free sweeteners that contain Xylitol can cause serious illness in a dog. Check the list of ingredients carefully when purchasing such products.

Tomatoes

This surprised me as my dogs have often had a slice of tomato from my plate or whilst I've been cooking. Although the question of tomatoes being toxic keeps popping up, you can be safely assured that they will not affect your dog.

Yeast Dough

Yeast dough has a rising agent in it that is not destroyed by heat during the baking process. Consequently, the dough could continue to ferment internally and cause wind, pain and possibly the rupture of internal organs. Small pieces of cooked bread given to a dog are fine as long as they do not replace a meal, but there are better foods for your pet. Why not try raw vegetables?

Plants in Your Garden

I make no apologies for adding plants to this chapter about toxic foods. Cala lilies, foxglove, crocus, narcissus and peonies in the garden, for example, are very toxic to pets and can kill. Others can cause mouth irritation and serious illness.

I for one try to keep my dogs away from the planted area of my garden. Not only can they trample and destroy valued flowers and plants, they often snuffle around in the earth and nibble at interesting discoveries. Once ingested, these new discoveries can cause upset tummies and worse. Bulbs may be dug up by inquisitive puppies and eaten with delight – dogs know no better! Keep an eye on your dog while enjoying your garden and check which plants are best removed out of harm's way.

Appendix 1
Oven Temperatures

How many times have you looked at a recipe only to find that it doesn't provide the correct type of oven temperature for your cooker? You have to stop cooking to convert the temperature provided which can be very infuriating.

Below is a guide to oven temperatures – use it as a guide only as ovens can vary considerably. You know your own cooker, so lower the setting if it cooks hotter than the norm. Fan assisted ovens cook faster so adjust the cooking times provided in recipes accordingly.

Aga, Rayburn and multi fuel stoves can also cook differently, so refer to the handbooks supplied with the cooker until you are used to the way they work.

°F	°C	Gas Mark	Oven Heat
225	110	¼	Very low
250	120/130	½	Very low
275	140	1	Low
300	150	2	Low
325	160/170	3	Medium
350	180	4	Medium
375	190	5	Medium/Hot
400	200	6	Medium/Hot
425	220	7	Hot
450	230	8	Very hot
475	240	9	Extremely hot

Appendix 2
Recommended Retailers and Books

Retailers
Manufacturer and supplier of herbal medicines
Dorwest Herbs Ltd
Shipton Gorge
Bridport
Dorset DT6 4LP
Tel: 01308 897272
Email: info@dorwest.com
Web: www.dorwest.com

Health supplements
Holland and Barrett Ltd
Online shopping: www.hollandandbarrett.com
Mail order: 0870 606 6606

Baking and kitchen equipment
Lakeland
Alexandra Buildings
Windermere
Cumbria LA23 1BQ
Tel: 01539 488100
Email: Contact form on website plus store locator
Web: www.lakeland.co.uk

The Cookie Cutter Shop
Web: www.thecookiecuttershop.com
(This is an online business.)

Cakes, Cookies and Crafts Shop
Morris Holbon Ltd
Unit 5, Woodgate Park
White Lund Industrial Estate
Morecambe
Lancashire LA3 3PS
Tel: 01524 389684
Email: Contact form on website
Web: www.cakescookiesandcraftsshop.co.uk

Books

What Vets Don't Tell You About Vaccines, Catherine O'Driscoll (First Stone). ISBN-10: 1929242492. ISBN-13: 978-1929242498.

Food Pets Die For: Shocking Facts About Pet Food, Ann N. Martin (NewSage Press). ISBN-10: 0939165562. ISBN-13: 978-0939165568.

Showing Your Dog: A Beginner's Guide, Elaine Everest (How To Books). ISBN-10: 1845283686. ISBN-13: 978-1845283681.

Index